Daughters of the Desert

Matilda Coxe Stevenson with Taos child. July 17, 1907.

Courtesy of the Smithsonian Institution.

DAUGHTERS OF THE DESERT

WOMEN ANTHROPOLOGISTS AND THE NATIVE AMERICAN SOUTHWEST, 1880–1980

AN ILLUSTRATED CATALOGUE

BARBARA A. BABCOCK
NANCY J. PAREZO

UNIVERSITY OF NEW MEXICO PRESS
ALBUQUERQUE

Library of Congress
Library of Congress Cataloging-in-Publication Data

Babcock, Barbara A., 1943–
Daughters of the desert: women anthropologists and the native American Southwest, 1880–1980: an illustrated catalogue / Barbara A. Babcock, Nancy J. Parezo.
p. cm.
Bibliography: p.
Includes index.
ISBN 0-8263-1087-7. ISBN 0-8263-1083-4 (pbk.)
1. Indians of North America—Southwest, New—Study and teaching—Exhibitions. 2. Anthropologists, Women—Southwest, New—Exhibitions. 3. Anthropology—Southwest, New—History—Exhibitions. I. Parezo, Nancy J. II. Title.
E78.S7B15 1988
979'.00497—dc19 88-2979
CIP

Second paperbound printing, 1990

Design: Milenda Nan Ok Lee

. . . let us admit we expect to be gathered up some day with the others as an exhibit in a Woman's Museum, a museum for collections of . . . the first law brief or first novel written by her, the first medical prescription signed or the first bone set by her, the first degree conferred upon her—exhibits which alone will be able to prove to a doubting posterity that once women were a distinct social class, the very special object of society's interest—for a variety of reasons.

—Elsie Clews Parsons
The Old-Fashioned Woman: Primitive Fancies about the Sex
(1913)

This business of women in anthropology is a perplexing one . . . a young woman, because of the likelihood of her marriage, is an unreliable element to build into the foundation of a staff structure.

—Letter from Alfred Kidder to Elsie Clews Parsons rationalizing the exclusion of women in the Laboratory of Anthropology's field schools, April 8, 1929.

Contents

Acknowledgments

This catalogue and the exhibit on which it is based have been supported by the Wenner-Gren Foundation for Anthropological Research, the Arizona Humanities Council, and the University of Arizona Foundation. Our thanks to their Boards and their Directors, Lita Osmundsen, Lorraine Frank, and Richard Imwalle for believing in this project. Our thanks also to SITES, the Smithsonian Institution Traveling Exhibit Service, for making the exhibit available to the national public. The Arizona State Museum and the Southwest Institute for Research on Women at the University of Arizona have sponsored this project, and we are especially grateful to Raymond H. Thompson, R. Gwinn Vivian, Myra Dinnerstein, and Janice Monk for their assistance and support. Our thanks to Deans Myles Brand and Richard Kinkade of the Colleges of Social and Behavioral Sciences and of Humanities of the University of Arizona for funding additional research assistance, and to chairmen William Stini and Edgar Dryden of the Departments of Anthropology and English who have also contributed to this project. Research and editorial assistants Mary Walker, Martha Brace, Jennifer Fox, Kelley Hays, Ruth Perry, and Barbara Slivac have been invaluable in collecting and editing immense amounts of materials. Sue Wolfe was especially essential in finding missing pieces and photographs and tying up loose ends. Our thanks, too, to Bruce Hilpert, Ernie Leavitt, Helga Teiwes, Diane Dittemore, Michael Jacobs, Kathy Hubenschmidt, Patricia Hollingshead, Steve Rogers, and Stuart Meehan who turned these materials into an exhibit. Sue Ruiz and George Sample of the Arizona State Museum provided indispensable clerical, secretarial, and logistical assistance. We are greatly indebted to the many individuals and institutions who have provided the information, photographs, and objects that made the exhibit and this catalogue possible. Our largest thanks, however, go to the five generations of women who have worked and are working as southwestern anthropologists and who have made this project both a necessity and a reality. Finally, our thanks to Elizabeth Hadas, Director of the University of New Mexico Press, who convinced us that it was essential to translate the exhibit into book form.

Daughters of the Desert

List of Abbreviations

AAA	American Anthropological Association
AAAS	American Association for the Advancement of Science
AES	American Ethnological Society
AFS	American Folklore Society
AID	Agency for International Development
APS	American Philosophical Society
BAE	Bureau of American Ethnology
BIA	Bureau of Indian Affairs
HEW	Department of Health, Education, and Welfare
JAF	*Journal of American Folklore*
MNA	Museum of Northern Arizona
NEA	National Endowment for the Arts
NIMH	National Institute of Mental Health
NPS	National Park Service
NRC	National Research Council
NSF	National Science Foundation
SAA	Society for American Archaeology
SAR	School of American Research
SSRC	Social Sciences Research Council
USGS	United States Geological Survey
USPHS	United States Public Health Service
WPA	Works Project Administration

Introduction

The harsh and limitless terrain of the American Southwest was frequently described as "no place for a lady," but it was to become a place where "ladies" thrived and created new identities for themselves as students and interpreters of the region's past and present Native American cultures. In 1878 William H. Holmes's *Report on the Ancient Ruins of Southwestern Colorado* announced to the scientific world the "rich rewards" awaiting archaeologists and ethnologists. The following year, Matilda Coxe Stevenson came to Hopi and Zuni as "volunteer coadjutor in ethnology" with the first collecting and research expedition of the newly formed Bureau of Ethnology. Since then, over 3,500 men and 1,600 women have followed in the path of those initial Smithsonian expeditions, making the Southwest the most studied region in anthropology. And just as surely as the land had shaped its indigenous cultures, this unconventional landscape with its very different ways of life, this "land of journey's ending," "bit sharply into the deep self" of the people who studied it (Austin 1924: 440).

"Restless and rebellious" women seeking freedom from their stays and from the drawing-room domesticity of Boston and New York found in the Southwest not only topographical and psychological space, but an otherness that intrigued and nurtured. By giving voice, visibility, and respect to disenfranchised Native Americans, hundreds of women made new lives for themselves. As scientists, humanists, romanticists, and activists, they were to significantly shape anthropological understandings, public conceptions, and government policies regarding the Native American Southwest. Since the turn of the century, when Alice Fletcher played a decisive role in locating the School of American Archaeology in Santa Fe and Matilda Coxe Stevenson set out "to do a comparatively complete and connected history of an aboriginal people whose thoughts are not our thoughts . . . [and] to erect a foundation upon which students may build" (Letter to John Wesley Powell, May 23, 1900), at least four generations of women have made distinctive contributions to the presentation, preservation, and appreciation of the pluralistic nature of southwestern society.

Poet and novelist Mary Austin wrote eloquently and endlessly about the "transactions" that took place between her spirit and the spirit of the land and its ancient peoples, but clearly she was not alone. If it is not surprising that so many women were drawn to the light and space of the Southwest and to "the minds and ways of its inhabitants," it is remarkable that they accomplished as much as they did, and it is very sobering indeed to contemplate what our understanding of this land and its people would be without them. Given the quality and quantity of their work, it is even more sobering to discover how notoriously displaced women are in official histories of southwestern anthropology, and how muted their distinctive meanings and explanations have become.

This catalogue and the exhibit on which it is based is part of an ongoing multi-faceted project which has also included a public conference, an oral history project and a prize-winning videotape, a scholarly conference and a book of essays, all of which were designed to generate a comprehensive assessment and re-vision of the role that women anthropologists and scholars, as well as artists, philanthropists, and activists have played in understanding and interpreting the Native American cultures of the Southwest during the past century. Despite the quantity and quality of women's work, we have little understanding of how their work influenced not only the development of American anthropological theory, but popular attitudes and government policies toward southwestern Native Americans. Neither do we know how important a factor gender has been and how the roles and opportunities available to women have influenced not only their research choices but how they have presented their work to the anthropological community and to the general public. Insofar as feminist method is understood to be "the collective critical reconstitution of the meaning of women's social experience, as women live through it" (MacKinnon 1982: 543), this project is a feminist endeavor "to recover our history and ourselves, each at least partly in terms of the other" (Chevigny 1983: 99).

We've coordinated these interrelated acts of re-membering the achievements and experiences of women in the Southwest under the title "Daughters of the Desert" not simply because of its alliterative properties and regional reference, but because we wanted to call attention to subordination in several figurative as well as literal and in several positive as well as negative senses. Many of the women who "set the trails" in the Southwest that countless other men and women anthropologists followed, were literally or figuratively the daughters of distinguished men who enabled either intellectually or financially. One cannot underestimate the role played in the development of southwestern anthropology by male scholars who were, in Ruth Bunzel's words, "hospitable to women and thought they had grey matter in their heads" (Interview, July 2, 1985). In archaeology, there was Dean Byron Cummings of the University of Arizona, who encouraged Clara Lee Tanner and Florence Hawley Ellis among others; and at the Museum of New Mexico, Edgar Lee Hewett who welcomed women, including Marjorie Lambert, Bertha Dutton, and Dorothy Keur to his field schools and excavations and was much criticized for doing so. In ethnology, there was Alfred Kroeber at Berkeley and Clyde Kluckhohn at Harvard, but before them and most importantly of all, there was Franz Boas at Columbia, affectionately described by his women students as "Papa Franz." As a German Jew, Boas experienced racism firsthand; as an anthropologist he believed "it is pertinent to ask whether any group has a rational basis for a claim to rights not accorded to others." And, as professor and chairman of anthropology at Columbia, he spent his career resisting authority, even his own. In 1920 he wrote to a colleague: "I have had a curious experience: All my best graduate students are women" (in Goldfrank 1978: 18). During his tenure there, over twenty women received Ph.D.s in anthropology, many of them doing fieldwork in the Southwest where their research, like Boas's own, was supported by Elsie Clews Parsons.

In describing the changes that American women such as Gertrude Stein, Nathalie Burney, and Sylvia Beach made in the artistic landscape of Paris between the Wars, Elaine Marks once suggested that "what every feminist needs is a wealthy dead father." And indeed, without several considerable New York and Boston fortunes inherited by women, the shape of southwestern studies would have been very different. In addition to Elsie Clews Parsons, there was Mary Hemenway, Mary Wheelwright, Mary Colton, Nathalie Curtis, Amelia White, and Millicent Rogers, to name but a few of the women who used their fathers' fortunes or family influence to finance expeditions, collections, field schools, research, and publications; to fight for Indian Rights and to support and encourage Indian arts and crafts; to persuade Theodore Roosevelt to lift the assimilationist ban against the singing and playing of Indian music; to lobby for the preservation of prehistoric ruins and for the establishment of national parks; and to build lasting and influential institutions such as the School of American Research, the Museum of Northern Arizona, the Wheelwright Museum, and the Millicent Rogers Museum.

Consider "daughters" in a second sense. In the past decade Virginia Woolf's assertion that "a woman writing thinks back through her mothers" has been frequently repeated as women scholars in a variety of disciplines have worked to recover their history and themselves by reconstructing and revising both the tradition and the individual stories of the women who preceded them—each of us wanting to know how other women "worked it out" or, as Ruth

N
NAVAJO
JICARILLA
APACHE
HAVASUPAI
HOPI
HOPI-TEWA
WALAPAI
RIO GRANDE
PUEBLOS
KERESAN
ZUNI
YAVAPAI
WESTERN
APACHE
RIVER
YUMAN
GILA PIMA
MARICOPA
MESCALERO
APACHE
CHIRICAHUA
APACHE
PAPAGO
CONCHO
OPATA
SERI
LOWER PIMA
TARAHUMARA
YAQUI
WARIJIO
MAYO
TEPEHUAN
Rio Fuerte
Rio Sinaloa
0 50 100 150
Miles

Benedict herself said of Mary Wollstonecraft, "I wanted so desperately to know how other women had saved their souls alive" (1959: 519). For over a century, women have distinguished themselves in anthropology, but most contemporary feminist anthropologists have been more concerned with women *in* culture than the women who wrote *about* culture and society. "Daughters of the Desert" was designed as a deliberate act of re-membering and re-viewing a long unexamined tradition in southwestern anthropology of women enabling and empowering other women, of women's texts engendering other women's texts—a matrilineage that has been suppressed and marginalized in "official" histories of anthropology and that far too few of us are aware of even though it has created the conditions of possibility that we enjoy today and authorized the work we do. Unlike many of the Indian peoples we study, we are not as aware as we might be of the extent to which one's status is determined by one's mother's clan. We hope that this project is the beginning of making the invisible visible, of tracing connections and genealogies, and of re-writing a story that needs re-telling.

There is "daughters" in a third sense. Many of us who work in this region are the fictive daughters not only of the women scholars who preceded us, but of the Native American women who have aided and befriended and shared their homes and their lives with us. As a consequence of this intimacy across cultural boundaries, many women have experienced a new sense of self and purpose. Chona, a Tohono O'Odham woman changed Ruth Underhill's life and she was not alone. Many women were literally given a new identity and new name by Indian women who adopted them into their clans. Elsie Clews Parsons had her hair washed at Hopi; Ruth Bunzel was adopted at Zuni; at Cochiti, Caroline Quintana washed Esther Goldfrank's hair and named her Abalone Shell; and when Bertha Dutton's mother died, Susie Marmon of Laguna adopted her.

Finally, there is the stark and spacious and uncompromising southwestern landscape that both dominates and frees all who live and work here. The emptiness of the west has been "a geography of possibility," a space of light and freedom and energy in which countless scholars, writers, and artists from Mary Austin to Elsie Clews Parsons to Georgia O'Keefe re-inscribed themselves. "The desert is no lady" and for that very reason it has nurtured the spirit of many independent women, including the poet, Pat Mora, who wrote those words. As naturalist Ann Zwinger recently remarked, "this quality and abundance of light cannot help but affect the way one sees" and writes about the world (1987: 146). And as Gertrude Stein wrote many years ago in a poem entitled "Landscape:"

> After all anybody is as their land and air is.
> Anybody is as the sky is low or high,
> the air heavy or clear
> and anybody is as there is wind or no wind there.
> It is that which makes them and the arts they make
> and the work they do and the way they eat
> and the way they drink
> and the way they learn and everything.
> (cited in Lander 1977: 194).

Less positively, women have been subordinated not only in the history of anthropology but, within the discipline, in terms of what they could and did study and write about. It is probably not accidental that much southwestern women's research has concentrated on arts and crafts, on culture and personality, on childrearing and acculturation, on music and literature. Or that despite the quality of the work they did, few women had "official" academic positions, many of them spending their lives in museums, which work anthropologist Clark Wissler saw as fitting for women since it resembled housekeeping. Even the strongest and most prolific of these women, such as Elsie Clews Parsons and Ruth Benedict, compartmentalized and compromised their discourse, wrote poetry under pseudonyms, and packed away their feminist writings under pressure to conform to male standards of "scientific" academic anthropology. Parsons was so teased about doing research in the summer and writing propaganda in the winter that, after many years of writing to educate the general public to the need for social freedom and equality, she wrote to anthropologist Robert Lowie in 1918: "You make the life of a psychologist not worth living. I see plainly I shall have to keep to the straight and narrow path of kinship nomenclature and folktale collecting" (cited in Hare 1985: 139); and, for the next twenty-two years she did just that. What might have they written if they had not subordinated their real selves? What did they write and never publish that we don't know about? How much has been buried and irretrievably so? Regrettably we have no choice but to read our history "into the scene of its own exclusion. It has, in other words, to be invented—both discovered and made up" (Kamuf 1982: 9).

This catalogue presents forty-five of these women and their work, concentrating on those women who began their careers before 1940 and who have worked primarily with the indigenous cultures of Arizona and New Mexico. The opening section introduces pioneers, Matilda Coxe Stevenson, Barbara Freire-Marreco Aitken, and Elsie Clews Parsons, who laid the foundation for Pueblo ethnographic studies and made a place for women in southwestern anthropology. The second section concentrates on women's research in four of the major cultures of the Southwest—Pueblo, Navajo, Papago, and Yaqui and the role that women have played in understanding the cultural diversity of the Native American Southwest. Women's contributions to the anthropological subfields of archaeology, applied anthropology, ethnomusicology, folklore, arts and crafts, and museology are documented in section three. This section also includes the efforts made by activists, popularizers, photographers, artists, and other "unofficial" anthropologists to preserve, record, and re-present the Native American Southwest. Throughout we have endeavored to let these women speak for themselves as much as possible in a patchwork of words and images. The text is accompanied with a selected southwestern bibliography of the featured women.

1 • Discovering the Southwest

The Southwest did not capture either the popular or the scientific imagination until the late 1870s, after the first photographic images were displayed at the Centennial in Philadelphia in 1876 and after the publication of the Smithsonian reports of Holmes, Stevenson, and Cushing. The combination of an open, unspoiled landscape and a settled, agrarian, highly developed Native American population made for a timeless, edenic image that contrasted sharply with the unhealthy, aggressive, industrial culture of the eastern and midwestern United States. As such, the region became the focus of economic and aesthetic as well as anthropological interest—places and peoples to be discovered, enjoyed, exploited, marketed, represented, and studied, particularly after the railroad reached New Mexico in 1880. Both as an alternative to masculine, industrial civilization and as an exotic but safe "laboratory" for the young science of anthropology, the Southwest became an important place for women. Before much money was available to anthropology or prestige associated with it, women were important in pioneering southwestern research and establishing the field. Matilda Coxe Stevenson was the first woman ethnographer to work in the Southwest and founded the Women's Anthropological Society to encourage and support women entering the field. Barbara Aitken was the first woman to challenge the "expedition mentality" of archaeology, to participate in a southwest field school, and to receive an advanced degree in anthropology. She was also a pioneer in combining archaeology and ethnography. Elsie Clews Parsons did monumental comparative research among the Pueblo, recognized the need to coordinate southwestern ethnological research, and through the Southwest Society which she founded in 1918, financed three critical decades of southwestern anthropological research and fieldwork by women as well as men.

Matilda Coxe Stevenson, ca. 1910.

"I want to do a comparatively complete and connected history of an aboriginal people whose thoughts are not our thoughts." (Letter to John Wesley Powell, May 23, 1900)

Courtesy of the American Anthropological Association.

MATILDA COXE STEVENSON, 1849–1915

"It is my wish to erect a foundation upon which students may build. I feel I can do the most for science in this way." (Letter to John Wesley Powell, May 23, 1900)

The first woman ethnographer to work in the Southwest, Matilda Coxe Stevenson, was a pioneer in the young science of anthropology. After graduating from a "sheltered female seminary" and studying law and geology, she accompanied her husband to Zuni in 1879 as a member of the first collecting and research expedition of the newly formed Bureau of Ethnology under the direction of John Wesley Powell. Assisting James Stevenson as "volunteer coadjutor in ethnology," Matilda collected information on women and family life and quickly developed a reputation as a vigorous and devoted scientist. She was the first American ethnologist to consider women and children worthy of notice and one of many unofficial women anthropologists whose writings were published largely under her husband's name.

Believing that ethnographic data must be collected before it was irretrievably lost, Matilda Coxe Stevenson concentrated on religion, which she regarded as the cornerstone of Pueblo culture and society. Her ethnographic studies at Zuni and at Sia, after her husband's death, were important beginnings, which did indeed become the foundation for future Pueblo research. In 1904 she began a monumental comparative study of Pueblo religion and spent the greater part of each year in New Mexico until her death in 1915.

EDUCATION: Private governesses, Miss Annable's Academy, Philadelphia, 1863–68; studied law with father, 1868; studied chemistry, mineralogy, and geology with Dr. N.M. Mew at Army Medical School of Washington, 1869–71.

RESEARCH: Geological surveys to Colorado, Idaho, Wyoming and Utah, 1872–78; ethnographic work with Ute and Arapaho, mid-1870s; ethnographic and museum collecting expeditions to Zuni and Hopi, 1879 and 1880, and to Rio Grande Pueblos, 1879; archaeological surveys in Arizona and California throughout 1880s; ethnographic fieldwork at Sia Pueblo, 1887–90; ethnographic work focusing on religion among Rio Grande Pueblos, 1904–15.

PROFESSIONAL ACTIVITIES: Law Clerk, 1868–72; accompanied husband on geological and anthropological expeditions as unpaid assistant, 1872–88; assisted husband prepare reports, analyses and catalogues of collections, 1879–88; Ethnologist, BAE, Smithsonian Institution, 1888–1915; Founder and President, Women's Anthropological Society of America, 1885; Judge, World's Columbian Exposition, 1893.

Zuni eating bowls collected by James and Matilda Stevenson in 1879. (Figures 428–430, *Illustrated Catalogue of the Collections Obtained from the Indians of New Mexico and Arizona in 1879*. Second Annual Report of the Bureau of Ethnology, 1883)

The Stevensons obtained over 33,000 ethnographic objects from Puebloan groups for the Smithsonian Institution. They concentrated on pottery, but also collected domestic objects, weapons, clothing, basketry, toys and musical instruments.

Courtesy of the Smithsonian Institution.

(*facing page*) *The Illustrated Police News* article on the Stevensons' trip to Oraibi, 1886.

Stevenson's crusading zeal in collecting data occasionally offended her subjects. In the late 19th century, however, her field methods were unfortunately the accepted practice.

Courtesy of the National Anthropological Archives, Smithsonian Institution.

COWED BY A WOMAN.

A Craven Red Devil Weakens in the Face of a Resolute White Heroine —Exciting Adventure in an Indian Village in Arizona.

Mar 6 '86

[Subject of Illustration.]

Col. James Stevenson of Washington, D. C., who has just returned from a six months' sojourn in collecting curiosities among the Indians of Arizona, was accompanied in his travels by Mrs. Stevenson, and the pair had an adventure among the Pueblo Indians quite unusual in its character. Having explored some newly discovered cave villages in the vicinity of Flagstaff, Ari., they gathered a small party and struck across the desert to the northeast for the Moqui towns, several days' journey distant. They arrived safely and encamped at the foot of a high mesa, upon the top of which stands Oreibe, the largest, western-most and least known of all the "Pueblo" towns. The people have a strong aversion to contact with the whites. Mr. and Mrs. Stevenson, accompanied by four friendly Moquis and as many Navajoes, rode into the village, dismounted and, climbing a ladder, ascended to the top of the high priest's house.

When the presence of the strangers became known there were signs of excitement throughout the village. The neighboring housetops and the plaza were thronged by excited barbarians, who chattered in loud voices and made threatening gestures. One burly savage upon a roof just above dangled a lariat suggestively noosed at the end, and loudly demanded that the whites be taken to the underground chapel of the village, and there summarily dealt with. One or two demonstrative individuals volunteered to be the first to apply the knife. The friendly Moquis stood their ground only a few minutes and then disappeared, but the Navajoes, who are made of firmer material, remained.

Col. Stevenson says that while the situation was highly interesting, it was probably less alarming than it would have been to people unacquainted with the natural timidity of the Pueblos. Mrs. Stevenson, who has sojourned with her husband among many wild tribes and knows the Indian character well, created an opportune diversion by shaking her fist in the face of a hunchbacked savage, whose vindictive eloquence seemed to exert a most mischievous influence over his fellows, addressing to him at the same time several brief but vigorous remarks in English and Spanish, which he was, of course, quite unable to understand. Before the man had recovered his self-possession, the strangers had backed down the ladder, and then slowly made their way, with the whole howling pack—men and women, children and dogs—at their heels, to their ponies, mounted and rode down to camp. They found the cook, who was the only other white person in the party, considerably alarmed. He said the camp was surrounded soon after their departure by many friendly Indians, but when the Moqui deserters reached them and told the story of the proceedings on the mesa, all mounted their ponies and made haste to get away. The cook feared his companions had been made prisoners, perhaps murdered.

HISTORICAL SKETCH

OF THE

WOMEN'S ANTHROPOLOGICAL SOCIETY

OF AMERICA.

BY

ANITA NEWCOMB MCGEE,

Recording Secretary.

READ AT THE ANNUAL RECEPTION, FEBRUARY 25, 1889.

On June 8, 1885, ten women of Washington met to form a scientific society. The idea was a novel one and hazardous, in that only one of the participants had ever done scientific work, to wit—Mrs. Tilly E. Stevenson. In her mind the plan of a women's anthropologic society was conceived, and to her energy, ability, and fostering care are due its birth and growth.

At the time of organization the objects of the Society were stated to be: "first, to open to women new fields for systematic investigation; second, to invite their coöperation in the development of the science of anthropology." The present constitution declares that "The object of this Society shall be to promote anthropology, by encouraging its study and facilitating the interchange of thought among those interested in anthropologic research, and by arranging and preserving systematically all information relating to it, and also by holding regular meetings for its discussion."

It is often asked why there should be two anthropologic societies in Washington. Speaking for ourselves, we have no desire to perpetuate a distinction of sex in science; and were we all professional scientists or possessed of education fitting us to enter the race for intellectual attainment without handicap, we doubt whether a second society would ever have been formed. Under existing conditions, however, we are satisfied to work out our own problems in antici-

Historical sketch of the Women's Anthropological Society of America, 1889.

Because the Anthropological Society of Washington refused to admit women, Stevenson founded the Women's Anthropological Society in 1885 to enable women to do research. The Society invited ". . . all who are clear in thought, logical in mental processes, exact in expression, and earnest in the search for truth, to make contributions of ascertained and properly related facts, and thus aid in the solution of the mighty problems that make up the humanity wide science of Anthropology." ("The Organization and Constitution of the Women's Anthropological Society," 1885.)

Courtesy of the National Anthropological Archives, Smithsonian Institution.

(*facing page*) Sandpainting and altar, Snake Society, Sia. (Plate XIV, from *The Sia* by Matilda Coxe Stevenson. Eleventh Annual Report of the Bureau of Ethnology, 1894.)

Although Stevenson began by studying the daily activities of women and children, she soon became more interested in Pueblo religion. After her husband's death in 1888, Matilda pursued her comparative study of Pueblo religion among the Rio Grande Pueblos.

Courtesy of Nancy Parezo and the Smithsonian Institution.

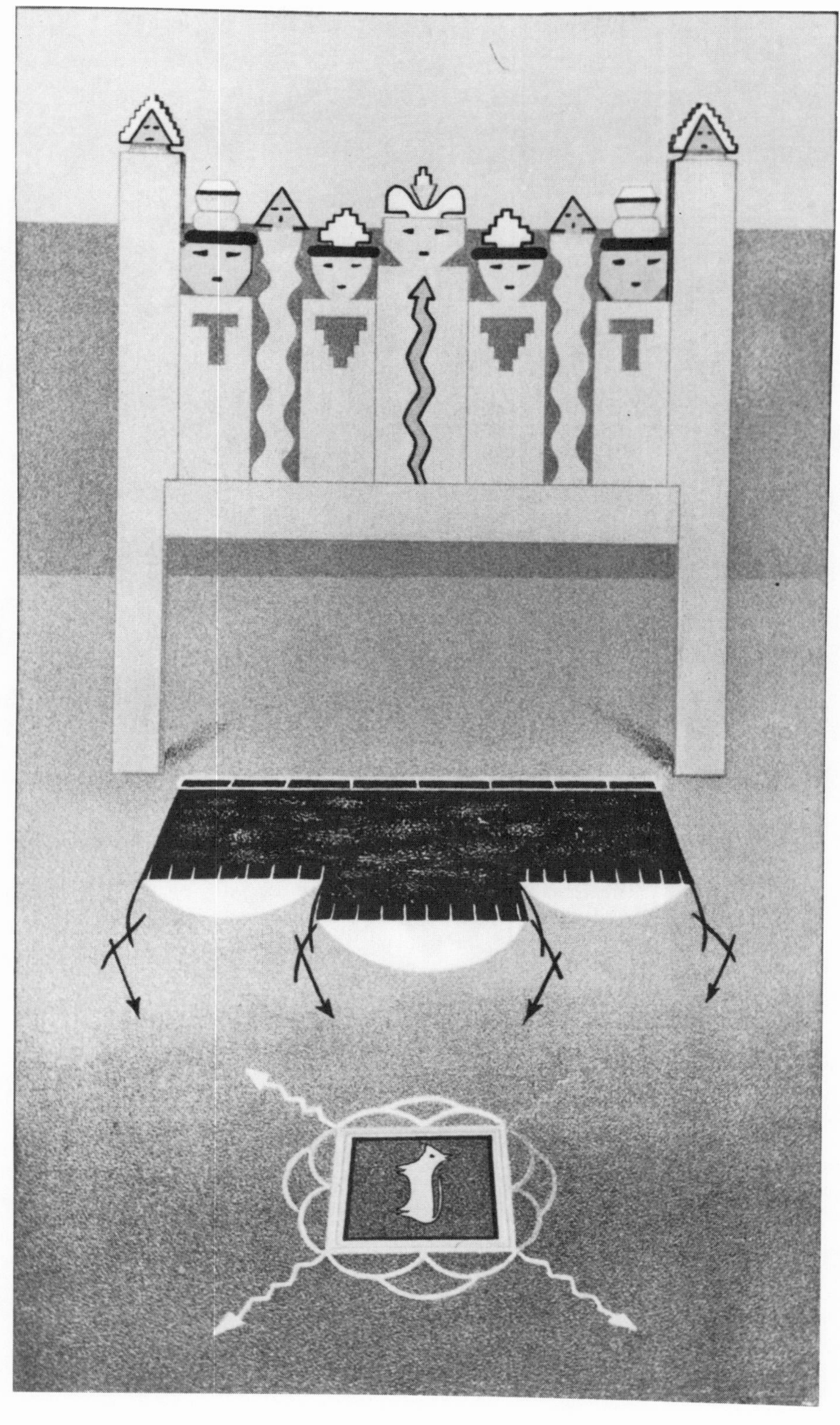

Elsie Clews Parsons, 1928.

"The *new woman* means the woman not yet classified, perhaps not classifiable, the woman *new* not only to men, but to herself." (*Social Rule,* 1916)

Courtesy of the American Philosophical Society.

Elsie Clews Parsons, 1875–1941

"Whether Indian or White one was fortunate indeed to live for a time in a world of such beauty." ("In the Southwest," n.d.)

The unconventional daughter of a Wall Street broker, early feminist sociologist and pacifist Elsie Clews Parsons turned her attention to anthropology after exploring the Southwest in 1910. On her first visit to Puye ruins, Parsons remarked "It is interesting to reconstruct cultures of ancient townbuilders, but more interesting to study the minds and ways of their descendants." ("In the Southwest," n.d.)

For the next 30 years, her dauntless spirit, inexhaustible energy, and incalculable wealth were dedicated to the study of Pueblo culture and society. She loved fieldwork and escaped to the Southwest as often as she could, returning "looking perfectly dreadful," her "disreputable" saddlebags filled with the stenographer's notebooks from which she produced a monumental series of monographs and articles (Lissa Parsons in Hare, *A Woman's Quest for Science,* 1985). In 1939, she published *Pueblo Indian Religion,* the comparative, encyclopedic synthesis that Stevenson had envisioned. Parsons provided intellectual direction and financial support for many anthropologists who worked in the Southwest during the 1920s and 1930s. She served as President of the American Folklore Society and the American Ethnological Society and was the first woman elected President of the American Anthropological Association. As a mentor and role model, she established a place for women in the field of anthropology. As Alfred Kroeber remarked, "Her society had encroached on her; she studied the science of society the better to fight back against society" (Spier and Kroeber, "Elsie Clews Parsons," 1943).

EDUCATION: B.A., Barnard College, 1896; M.A., Columbia University, 1897; Ph.D., sociology, Columbia University, 1899.

FELLOWSHIPS AND AWARDS: Hartley House Fellow, Barnard College, 1899–1902.

RESEARCH: Zuni, 1915; Zuni and Laguna, 1917–18; Laguna, 1919; Hopi, Acoma, Laguna, Isleta, and Taos Pueblos, 1916–32; Pima, 1926; Kiowa and Caddo, 1927; Cahitan groups in Sonora, 1932; Mitla, Oaxaca, 1929–33; Ecuador, 1940–41; folklore collecting trips to black communities in American South and West Indies.

PROFESSIONAL ACTIVITIES: Lecturer in sociology, Barnard College, 1902–05; graduate courses on the family and on sex roles at Columbia University, 1902–05, New School for Social Research, 1919; founds Southwest Society in 1918 to co-ordinate and support southwestern research; Treasurer, 1916–22, President, 1923–25, Vice-president, 1933–35, AES; Assistant Editor, *JAF,* 1918–41; President, AFS, 1918–20; Council, AAA, 1923–26; Vice-president, AFS, 1932–34; Board, Laboratory of Anthropology, 1935; Vice-president, 1927–29, President, 1940–41, AAA.

Parsons at San Gabriel Ranch, Alcalde, New Mexico, ca. 1913.

After her first trip to the Southwest in 1910, Parsons returned regularly, frequently staying with Clara True who "much disapproved" of Parsons' "habits of smoking and wearing riding-breeches." ("In the Southwest," n.d.)

Courtesy of the American Philosophical Society.

Zuni N M.

Dec.3.1919.

Dear Lady Mine;

Near as I can count now Leskwe will begin the 19 and end the 30th. It is so hard to get the exact time. Some want the Paquin to count the way the other Paquin did and some want some other way .If they change the time other than I have counted I will wire you.

Today is the last of the Shalico.They are going away. I was called home to Okla.by the death of my mother and as I was on my way back I fell acoross the railroad track and hurt my shin.very bad;I have not been able to put my foot to the floor :My leg was so swollen I could not wear my shoe. I am able to be up on it now but it is not healed yet.This rest at Shalico has been a god send to me and I think I will be able to teach Monday.

We had about six inches of snow Shalico night and it is awful muddy but not very cold.

Will be glad to see you if you can come.

Let me know if you cancome so I can prepare for you.

Love from

Margaret L.

Margaret Lewis, Parsons' friend and hostess at Zuni, writing to tell her about upcoming ceremonies in 1919.

Margaret Lewis told Loki Pandey that Parsons "was a real friend of my husband and me. We always wrote to each other. . . . Although she was very talkative, we enjoyed having her with us and she was also glad for that." (Quoted in "Anthropologists at Zuni," 1972)

Courtesy of the American Philosophical Society and *Desert Magazine*.

Dec 26, 1925

SAN GABRIEL RANCH
Alcalde, New Mexico

Dear Dr. Sapir:

Mr. White sounds promising, and the South West Society will be glad to finance a field trip for him. We have found that $700 - $800 about covers expenses. I suppose he would plan it for next summer. He might try a survey of the social organization of Acoma, which should be an interesting link between the Keres and Zuñi. Nothing published except one slight article by myself as observation during a short visit. Since then we have completed surveys of several other towns, so that White would have a considerable amount of comparative material.

Yours faithfully
Elsie Clews Parsons

[to E. Sapir, 12-26-'25]

(*left*) Letter to Edward Sapir regarding Leslie White's southwest research, December 26, 1925.

Through the Southwest Society which she established in 1918, Parsons funded the research and publications of most of the anthropologists who worked in the Southwest in the 1920s and 1930s.

Courtesy of the University of Michigan.

(*facing page, top*) "Isleta Dance" from *Isleta Paintings*, February 29, 1939.

"To describe even a part of a culture is a dangerous enterprise, so interwoven is one part with another that the fabric tears when we begin to separate, leaving meaningless shreds in our hands. This is particularly true of those values and forms we call religion." (*Pueblo Indian Religion*, 1939)

Between 1936 and 1941, Parsons received 140 drawings documenting Isleta social and ceremonial life from Joe B. Lente, an untutored artist. Two decades after Parsons' death, Esther Goldfrank completed her preparations for publication.

Courtesy of the American Philosophical Society.

(*facing page, bottom*) Musical instruments used in Pueblo ritual dances.

"Religion is an instrument of life." (*Pueblo Indian Religion*, 1939)

(*left to right*)
Tesuque drum, ca. 1950. Arizona State Museum, Cat. No. 81-15-8.

Taos flute, pre-1950. Arizona State Museum, Cat. No. GP 52635.

Rio Grande Pueblo turtle shell rattle, pre-1926. Arizona State Museum, Cat. No. GP 4364.

Jemez gourd rattle, ca. 1960. Arizona State Museum, Cat. No. E-7775.

Photograph by Helga Teiwes. Courtesy of the Arizona State Museum.

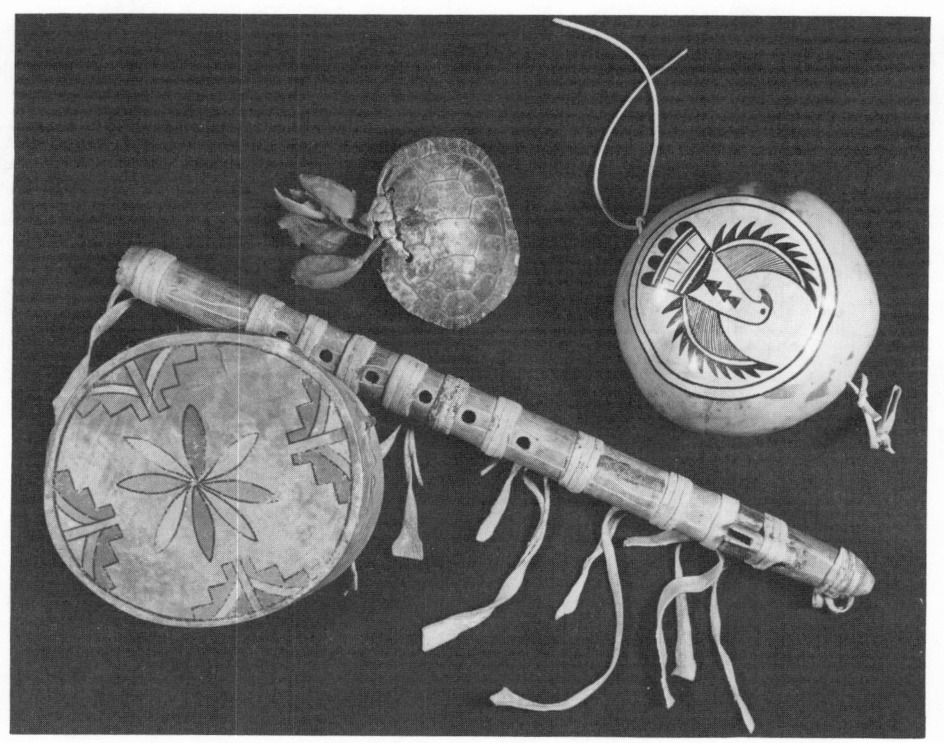

Oxford's first anthropology diploma students with Henry Balfour, 1908. (*left to right*) F.H.S. Knowles, Henry Balfour, Barbara Freire-Marreco, A. Hadley.

"I think Dr. Parsons misunderstood Hano to some extent. So did I . . . I was living too much in corn-people's pocket." (Letter to Edward Dozier, July 5, 1954)

Courtesy of the Pitt Rivers Museum, Oxford.

Barbara Freire-Marreco Aitken, 1879–1967

"Would I could see it again, those wonderful transparent coloured distances, but the remembrance of it is a lasting joy!"
(Letter to Edward Dozier, July 5, 1954)

In 1908, Barbara Freire-Marreco took a diploma in anthropology with distinction, a member of the first class of anthropology students to graduate from Oxford. From 1909 to 1913 she held the Somerville Research Fellowship. After a summer at Edgar Lee Hewett's Frijoles Canyon field school in 1910, her principal research was with the Tewa of Santa Clara and Hano Pueblos. She lived in these villages for extensive periods between 1910 and 1913, where she was remembered with affection and awe for her remarkable knowledge of the Tewa language and native customs.

The shift in Freire-Marreco's research interests from archaeology to ethnography was prompted both by Hewett's desire for information on the living inhabitants of the Pajarito Plateau and by the difficulties that a single woman in a 1910 field school presented. After returning to England, she lectured at the London School of Economics until 1923, when she married Robert Aitken and left her London circle for Hampshire.

EDUCATION: B.A., diploma in anthropology, Oxford University, 1907; M.A., anthropology, Oxford University, 1920.
FELLOWSHIPS AND AWARDS: Research Fellow, Oxford University, 1901–13; Mary Ewart Travelling Scholar, Somerville College, Oxford University, 1912–13.
RESEARCH: Archaeology with Edgar Lee Hewett at Rito de los Frijoles, 1910; ethnographic and linguistic research at Santa Clara and Hano Pueblos, 1910–13; ethnographic fieldwork with Yavapai, 1913; fieldwork on agriculture, linguistics, folklore in Spain, 1926, 1930, 1932.
PROFESSIONAL ACTIVITIES: Lecturer, London School of Economics, 1911, 1929; Editor, *Notes and Queries in Anthropology* for British Association for the Advancement of Science, 1912–29; Secretary, Barnett House, Oxford University, 1917; editorial staff, War Trade Intelligence Department, 1916–18; Resident Scholar and Member of Council, Lady Margaret Hall, Somerville College, Oxford University, 1920–23; President, University of London Anthropological Society, 1928; Secretary of various anthropological societies in Great Britain in 1920s; discussant of papers on North American Indians, writer of extensive reviews and short articles on varied customs and ceremonies for several British societies and journals, especially *Folk-lore,* 1920–60.

Barbara Aitken at Hewett's field school in Frijoles Canyon, 1910. (*left to right, front row*) Sylvanus G. Morley, Kenneth M. Chapman, J.P. Adams, Jesse Nusbaum, Nate Goldsmith, Junius Henderson. (*standing*) Wilfred Robbins, Donald Beauregard, John P. Harrington, Frederick W. Hodge, Edgar Lee Hewett, Neil Judd, Miss Woy, Barbara Freire-Marreco Aitken.

Courtesy of the Museum of New Mexico.

Santa Clara Pueblo Council Members. (*left to right*) Santiago Naranjo, Manuel Tafoya, Leandro Tafoya, Victoriano Cisneros.

Of Santiago Naranjo, then Governor of the Pueblo, Aitken later recalled to Edward Dozier: "He would tell me frankly if I were approaching a forbidden subject: 'that, friend, is important' and put me on my honor to ask no further questions of himself or of less scrupulous informants." (Aitken/Dozier Papers, Arizona State Museum Archives, A-0869)

Photograph by Barbara Freire-Marreco Aitken. Courtesy of the Arizona State Museum.

2. • UNDERSTANDING CULTURAL DIVERSITY

By 1910, the basic ethnographic mapping of the Southwest was completed and the groundwork laid for future investigations. In contrast to the almost exclusive focus on Puebloan peoples that had dominated the early years of southwestern anthropology, researchers began to investigate other Indian cultures and to amass comparative materials. Between 1910 and 1945, a "salvage" attitude accompanied by the compiling of facts and the inventorying of cultural traits was replaced by an awareness of the complexity of southwest culture history and an interest both in diffusion and in the linguistic, cultural, and topographical diversity of the Southwest. Concern with and investigation of the principles of social integration and cultural patterns and configurations produced much finer-grained analyses and a picture of southwest Indian societies as distinctive organized wholes.

Women's research, like that of southwestern anthropology in general, was initially focused on the Pueblos because they were approachable, because of the continuity and intactness of their culture, because Parsons herself studied these peoples and encouraged and funded others' investigations of the same, and, perhaps most importantly, because the "peaceful" Pueblo were deemed safe for women. The nomadic Navajo were less "settled" and accessible, the desert environment of the Papago and the Yaqui was harsh and inhospitable, and the Apache much too hostile and recently subdued. The Apache wars were not over until 1886 and the killing of Columbia student Henrietta Schmerler on the Fort Apache Reservation in the summer of 1931 had predictable consequences: virtually no women have worked with Apachean groups other than the Mescalero. With the exception of the Apache, women have, however, made notable and primary contributions to the understanding of the cultural diversity of the Southwest.

PUEBLO

Prior to 1930, southwestern anthropologists focused their attention on the pueblos of northern New Mexico and Arizona. In an age of dirt roads and Model T Fords, these large permanent villages were the most accessible of southwestern cultures. Both ethnologists and archaeologists were drawn to the "ancient ways of life" embodied in rich ceremonial and aesthetic traditions and inscribed in countless ruins.

Following Parsons's lead and funded by her Southwest Society, many of Boas's students at Columbia University went west in the 1920s to do their first fieldwork among the Pueblo. Women scholars such as Ruth Benedict, Ruth Bunzel, and Esther Goldfrank soon achieved prominence in twentieth-century anthropology, as did native Arizonan and Chicago graduate, Florence Hawley Ellis, who combined ethnology and archaeology.

Ruth Benedict in her office at Columbia University, ca. 1940.

"I haven't the strength of mind not to need a career." (*An Anthropologist at Work,* 1959)

Photograph by Helen Codere. Courtesy of the Vassar College Library.

Ruth Benedict, 1887–1948

"A culture, like an individual, is a more or less consistent pattern of thought and action."
(*Patterns of Culture,* 1934)

In 1919, Ruth Benedict enrolled in Elsie Clews Parsons' "Sex in Ethnology" course at the New School for Social Research. This restless and rebellious poet shared Parsons' concern with the relationship between individual creativity and cultural constraints. Two years later, she received a Ph.D. from Columbia University and began her distinguished career in anthropology as Boas's assistant and colleague. Benedict's feminist perspective and advocacy of cultural relativity had a decisive influence on the careers of Margaret Mead, Ruth Underhill, and Ruth Bunzel.

Although hampered by deafness, Benedict did significant fieldwork in collecting myths and tales at both Zuni and Cochiti Pueblos. Pueblo culture appealed to her configurational perspective which was developed and presented in *Patterns of Culture* (1934). This book introduced a humanistic and interdisciplinary approach to the study of society, and remains the single most popular and influential work by a twentieth-century anthropologist.

EDUCATION: B.A., English, Vassar College, 1909; graduate studies, New School for Social Research, 1919–21; Ph.D., anthropology, Columbia University, 1923.

FELLOWSHIPS AND AWARDS: Southwest Society grants, 1924, 1925, 1927; American Design Award, 1946; Achievement Award, American Association of University Women, 1946; Doctor of Science, Russell Sage College, 1947.

RESEARCH: Ethnographic fieldwork: Morongo Valley, Serrano, 1922; Zuni Pueblo, 1924, 1925, 1927; Cochiti Pueblo, 1925; Pima, 1927; Mescalero Apache, 1931; Blackfoot, Alberta, Canada, 1939.

PROFESSIONAL ACTIVITIES: Teacher, Westlake School for Girls, Los Angeles, 1911–12; Teacher, Orton School for Girls, Pasadena, 1912–14; Teaching Assistant to Franz Boas, Barnard College, 1922–23; Lecturer in Anthropology, 1923–30, Assistant Professor to Professor, 1930–1948, Columbia University; AAA Council, 1924–27, 1931–47; Secretary-Treasurer, AES, 1931; President, AES, 1927–29; Editor, *JAF,* 1928–39; Director, Summer Field Trip, Apache, Laboratory of Anthropology, 1931; Member, Kardiner-Linton seminars on anthropology and psychoanalysis, 1936–39; Director, Summer Field Trip, Blackfoot, 1939; Anna Howard Shaw Memorial Lecturer, Bryn Mawr, 1941; Member, Committee on Food Habits, NRC, 1941–44; Member, Institute for Intercultural Studies, 1941–44; Social Scientist, Office of War Information, 1942–46; Fellow, Washington School of Psychiatry, 1945; Vice-President, American Psychopathological Association, 1946; Member, Committee on Research of the Office of Naval Research, 1946–48; Assistant Editor, *Psychiatry,* 1946; Program Chair, AAA, 1938; Vice-President, AAA, 1938–43; President, AAA, 1947; Committee on Standards of Professional Status, Representative to NRC, 1946; Editorial Board, *American Scholar;* Editor, *Columbia University Contributions to Anthropology;* Director, Research on Contemporary Cultures, 1947–48.

(*above*) Ruth Benedict, Franz Boas, and Alfred Kroeber at an anthropology picnic, ca. 1920.

"I have had a curious experience in graduate work during the last few years. All my best students are women." (Letter from Boas to Berthold Laufer, July 23, 1920)

Photograph by Esther Goldfrank. Courtesy of the National Anthropological Archives, Smithsonian Institution.

(*bottom right*) Hopi Snake Dance Figurine, ca. 1920. Arizona State Museum, Cat. No. E-4750.

"Their culture has not disintegrated like that of all the Indian communities outside of Arizona and New Mexico. Month by month and year by year, the old dances of the gods are danced in their stone villages, life follows essentially the old routines." (*Patterns of Culture,* 1934)

Photograph by Helga Teiwes. Courtesy of the Arizona State Museum.

Edward Sapir at New Haven, Connecticut, 1936–37 and a poem which he sent to Benedict in 1926.

Courtesy of Philip Sapir.

Zuni

I send you this. Through the monotony
Of mumbling melody, the established fall
And rise of the slow, dreaming ritual,
Through the dry glitter of the desert sea
And sharpness of the mesa keep the flowing
Of your spirit, in many branching ways,
Be running mirrors to the colored maze,
Not pool enchanted nor a water slowing.

Hear on the wing, see in a flash, retreat!
Beauty is brightest when the eye is fleet.
And priests are singing softly on the sand
And the four colored points and zenith stand;
The desert crawls and leaps, the eagle flies.
Put wax into your ears and close your eyes.

(Edward Sapir. Reprinted in *An Anthropologist at Work,* 1959).

Words in Darkness

There will come beauty in a silver rain
Out of the storm-hung heaven of my soul.
Let me remember seasons that have lain
Heavy as this with darkness and the roll
Of the on-coming thunder, and were yet
Distilled to showers crystal-cool and white
Beyond the gift of sunshine; heedless, let
The storm close cold upon me, and the bite
Of sand be on my breasts, nor question why
The silver fingers of the rain are wrought
Out of a maddened tumult and a sky
No man of all would willingly have sought.

(*Selected Poems,* 1941. Reprinted in *An Anthropologist at Work,* 1959).

Benedict published poetry under the pseudonym Anne Singleton. She and linguist Edward Sapir shared interests in anthropology, poetry, and psychology, and maintained a lively correspondence, exchanging poems. Sapir regarded her "poeticizing" as more important than her "anthropologizing," and admonished her when she did not "send verses." (*An Anthropologist at Work,* 1959)

(*above left*) Santiago Quintana, Cochiti storyteller, ca. 1925.

(*above right*) Storyteller figurine by Helen Cordero, 1980.

Helen Cordero's grandfather was well known in the pueblo as a gifted storyteller and leading member of one of the clown societies. In addition to entertaining countless Cochiti children, Santiago Quintana was friend and informant to several generations of students of Cochiti life: Adolph Bandelier, Frederick Starr, Charles Saunders, Edward Curtis, Elsie Clews Parsons, and Ruth Benedict.

Photograph by Edward S. Curtis. Courtesy of Barbara Babcock.

In 1964, Helen Cordero made the first of many Storytellers depicting her grandfather, Santiago Quintana, who was Benedict's favorite narrator. "My old man is ninety and a great old character. . . . He hobbles along on his cane, bent nearly double, and is still easily the most vivid personage in the landscape—he has the habit of enthusiasm and of good fellowship." (Letter from Benedict to Mead, September 5, 1925. Reprinted in *An Anthropologist at Work*, 1959)

Courtesy of Barbara Babcock. Composite photograph by Helga Teiwes. Courtesy of the Arizona State Museum.

Official Opening of the Laboratory of Anthropology and Pecos Conference, September 1, 1931.

Ruth Benedict was the first woman to direct one of the Laboratory of Anthropology's field schools in ethnology. In the summer of 1931, Benedict and her students, who included Paul Frank, Morris Opler, Sol Tax, Harry Hoijer, Jules Blumensohn, and Regina Flannery, lived and worked with Mescalero Apache families.

(*left to right*) John McGregor, "Uncle Benny" Hyde, Frank H.H. Roberts, Neil M. Judd, Kenneth Chapman, W.W. Postlethwaite, Emil W. Haury, A.V. Kidder, Anna O. Shepard, Arthur Woodward, Marjorie Trumbull, W.S. Stallings, Jesse L. Nusbaum, Paul H. Nesbitt, Mrs. R.B. Alves, Ralph L. Roys, Paul Martin, Clark Wissler, Dr. Van Bergen, George Woodbury, Byron Cummings, J.A. Jeancon, Lyndon Hargrave, Dale King, R.D. Brown, Carl Miller, Sol T. Kimball, Ruth Benedict, Henry Roberts, Paul Frank, Alice R. Stallings, Harry P. Mera, Stanley Stubbs, Charles Amsden.

Courtesy of the Museum of New Mexico.

Esther Goldfrank at Laguna, 1921.

"My entry into the Southwest was accidental, but the data had an interest and I think I utilized it as far as I was able under the circumstances and the shortness of my visit." (Interview, July 3, 1985)

Courtesy of the National Anthropological Archives, Smithsonian Institution.

Esther Goldfrank, 1896–

"I'm a realist, not an idealist. I never had a thesis, I just took the facts and let them fall where they may." (Interview, July 3, 1985)

Barnard College graduate Esther Goldfrank became Boas's secretary in 1919. Her salary and subsequent southwestern field trips were financed by Elsie Clews Parsons. In June of 1920, Goldfrank went to Laguna Pueblo with Boas and Parsons, and began her fieldwork eliciting cooking recipes from a Laguna woman. In 1921 and 1922, she accompanied Boas to Cochiti Pueblo and here, too, her "helpers were a group of women—by and large it was a woman's party." Goldfrank's collaboration with Caroline Quintana, mother of now-famous potter Helen Cordero, resulted in *The Social and Ceremonial Organization of Cochiti* (1927).

Although she never received a degree in anthropology, Esther Goldfrank has made significant contributions to Pueblo studies. From her "realist" perspective, she challenged Benedict's "Apollonian" characterization of Pueblo culture. With husband Karl Wittfogel, she wrote several essays detailing the importance of irrigation for Pueblo social and ceremonial organization. In 1962, Goldfrank completed and published Parsons' work on *Isleta Paintings*.

EDUCATION: B.A., Barnard College, 1918; graduate study in anthropology, Columbia University, 1921–22, 1937.

FELLOWSHIPS AND AWARDS: Grants from Southwest Society, 1920, 1921, 1922, 1924.

RESEARCH: Ethnographic fieldwork at Laguna Pueblo, 1920–21; Cochiti Pueblo, 1921–22; Isleta Pueblo, 1924; Blackfoot Reservation, Alberta, Canada, 1939.

PROFESSIONAL ACTIVITIES: Secretary and Research Assistant to Franz Boas, Columbia University and Southwestern Pueblos, 1919–22; Researcher, Rockefeller Foundation, General Education Board Study of Adolescents, 1936–38; Member, Kardiner-Linton Seminars in psychoanalysis and anthropology, 1938–39; Staff Anthropologist, Chinese History Project, Columbia University, 1945ff.; AAA Council, 1925–29, 1946; Secretary-Treasurer, 1946–48, President, 1948, AES; Fellow, AAA; Fellow, New York Academy of Sciences.

Franz Boas, Solomon Day and Karl Leon climbing Mt. Taylor, New Mexico, 1921.

Boas's Pueblo research was encouraged and financed by Elsie Clews Parsons, who joined him and Goldfrank at Laguna in 1920. He dedicated *Keresan Texts* (1928) to Parsons "as a slight expression of gratitude for [her] energetic and unselfish labors that have brought about a revival of interest in Southwestern ethnology."

Photograph by Esther Goldfrank. Courtesy of the National Anthropological Archives, Smithsonian Institution.

Caroline Quintana, Cochiti, 1921.

"She did live near the plaza she said and she asked me if I would like to visit her. It was not too long before I told her I was interested in learning kinship terms." (*Notes on an Undirected Life,* 1978)

Photograph by Esther Goldfrank. Courtesy of Barbara Babcock.

17 m. Santiato Quintana (bawεtε) Squash
+18 F. Sepherina Garcia (cratεmε) Oak

- 6 m. Pablo Quintana (wapurn^{y}i) Oak
  - +76* F. Petra Herrara (gatsia)Water
    - 71 F. Carmelita Quintana (curdjuminako) Water
    - 73 F. Lupeta Quintana (ma'wenatsa) Water
  - +1 F. Caroline Trujillo (ayo´witsa) Fox
    - 7 F. Trinidad Quintana (o´cala) Fox
    - 8 F. Helen Quintana (d^{y}aiyrowitsa) Fox
- 19 F. Stephana Quintana (creitiatsa) Oak
  - +38* m. Francisco Quintana (hawelinɑ) Turquoise
    - 24 m. Damacio Quintana (koole) Oak
    - 25 m. Iskibula Quintana (cpula) Oak
    - 26 m. Jerome Quintana (kaega´) Oak
- +27 m. Antonio kallebassa (tsinaut') Cipewe
- 20 F.. Victoria Quintana (ts'ɑ´m^{ue}) Oak
  - +28 m. Adelaido Monotoya (tsi´watεla) Cottonwood.
    - 29 F. Aurelio Montoya (dza´ditsa) Oak
    - 30 m. Celso Montoya (ca´wadiwa) Oak
- 21 F. Rais Quintana (kε´wi) Oak
  - +39 m. Vicente Romero (ayolis) Sage
    - 40 F. Juanita Romero (naweditsa) Oak
    - 41 F. Laurencita Romero (tsaca^{y}latsa) Oak
    - 42 F. Katherine Romero (a^{y}atεatsɑ) Oak
    - 43 F. Profilia Romero (d^{y}εtsi) Oak
    - 44 F. Lucia Romero (waamotsa) Oak
- 22 F. Criscencia Quintana (tsεiatsɑ) Oak
  - +45 m. Cliofi Arquero (maic´^{e}) Sage
    - 46 m. Evelino Arquero (k'oyo) Oak
- 23 m. Jose Dominto Quintana (cakak) Oak
  - +47 F. Domingita Quintana (crityaya) Cottonwood
    - 48 m. Sylviana Quintana (d^{y}an^{y}i) Cottonwood
    - 49 m. Delphine Quintana (wi´ctowi) Cottonwood
    - 50 m. Benito Quintana (loquimur) Cottonwood

Genealogical chart of Quintana family from *Social and Ceremonial Organization of Cochiti*, 1927.

Goldfrank lived with Pablo and Caroline Quintana while working at Cochiti. From them she collected much of the data on which her monograph is based.

Courtesy of the American Anthropological Association. Photograph by Helga Teiwes. Courtesy of the Arizona State Museum.

Pablo and Caroline Quintana with their daughter Helen, Cochiti, 1921.

Famous figurative potter Helen Cordero was six years old when Esther Goldfrank lived with her family.

Photograph by Esther Goldfrank. Courtesy of Barbara Babcock.

Ruth Bunzel, 1985.

"I felt there was a great lack of knowledge about peoples' lives—particularly about women—so being a woman, that was the obvious place to start." (Interview, July 2, 1985)

Courtesy of the Wenner-Gren Foundation.

RUTH BUNZEL, 1898–

"Fieldwork requires both men and women to really get a whole picture of culture." (Interview, July 2, 1985)

Ruth Bunzel, another Barnard graduate, succeeded Esther Goldfrank as Boas's secretary and editorial assistant in 1922. Like Goldfrank, she was drawn to the Southwest and became increasingly involved with anthropology. In the summer of 1924, Bunzel wanted to "try a bit on [her] own" to decide if she "wanted to be and could be an anthropologist." (Interview, July 2, 1985) Instead of accompanying Boas to Europe, she met Ruth Benedict in Zuni.

Boas "wanted someone to look at the relation of the artist to his work," so Bunzel apprenticed herself to Zuni potters. (Interview, July 2, 1985) Her "indirect" approach to art from the Zuni point of view was innovative, and *The Pueblo Potter* (1929) became a landmark in Pueblo ethnoaesthetic studies. Like Cushing and Benedict, Bunzel also contributed significantly to the study of Zuni mythology and ritual poetry.

EDUCATION: B.A., Barnard College, 1918; Ph.D., anthropology, Columbia University, 1929. Attended University of Chicago, 1928.

FELLOWSHIPS AND AWARDS: SSRC, 1927–29; Rockefeller Foundation, 1927–29; Guggenheim Foundation, 1930–32.

RESEARCH: Fieldwork focusing on religion and aesthetics at Zuni Pueblo, beginning 1924; in Mexico, Guatemala, Spain, and among the Chinese in New York City.

PROFESSIONAL ACTIVITIES: Secretary and Editorial Assistant to Franz Boas, Columbia University, 1922–24; Lecturer, Barnard College, 1929–30; Lecturer, 1933–41, 1953–60, Adjunct Professor, 1960–69, Senior Research Associate, 1969–87, Columbia University; Social Scientist, U.S. Office of War Information, Washington, 1942–45; Associate Director, Research in Contemporary Cultures, 1947–51; Chair, Section H, AAAS, 1974–76; Auditor, 1936, Secretary-Treasurer, AES; Executive Committee Board, AAA, 1928–1943.

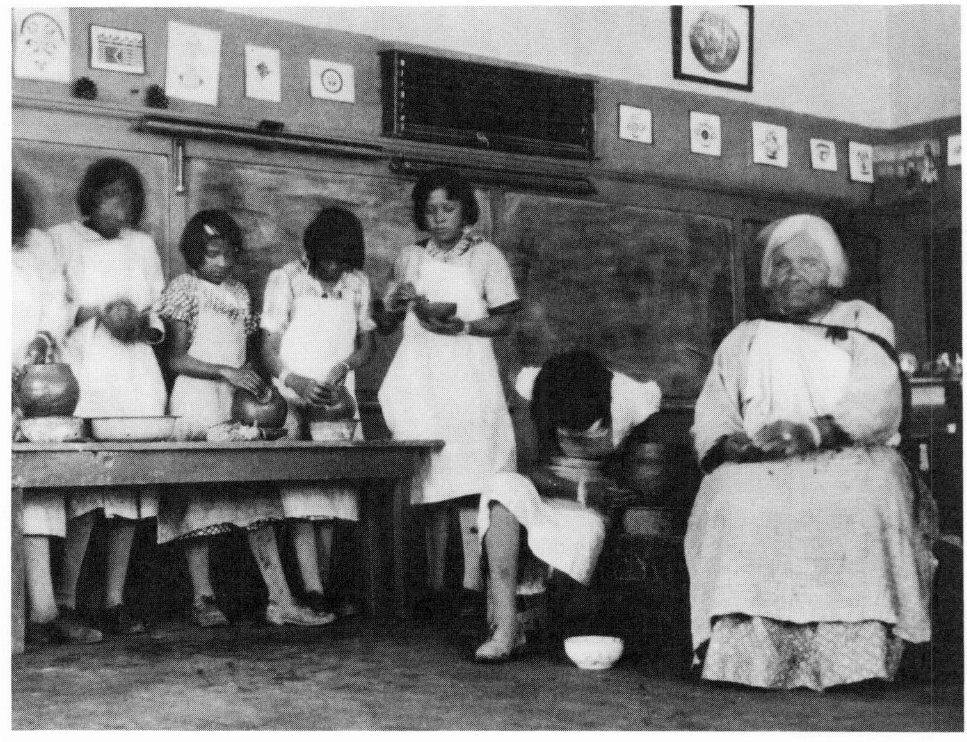

Zuni pottery designs from *The Pueblo Potter* (1929).

Bunzel's approach to the Zuni potters' "patient pursuit of perfection" changed the study of tribal arts. As she later told Margaret Mead, "I was too ignorant at the time to know that I was pioneering; that I was on the frontier of a whole new field of anthropology." (Quoted in Mead, "Apprenticeship under Boas," 1959)

Courtesy of Dover Publications.

(*facing page, top*) Sacred Mesa with Shalako Dancers in foreground, Zuni, 1957.

"Ruth Bunzel came by Friday's mail wagon. Yesterday we went up under the sacred mesa along stunning trails where the great wall towers above you always in new magnificence. . . . When I'm God I'm going to build my city there." (Letter from Ruth Benedict to Margaret Mead, August 24, 1925. Reprinted in *An Anthropologist at Work,* 1959)

Courtesy of the Arizona State Museum.

(*facing page, bottom*) Catalina Zunie teaching a pottery class, 1934.

For many years Bunzel worked with Catalina Zunie, who taught many Zuni children to make pottery. "Zuni is a woman's society. The women have a great deal of power and influence, so it's a good place for women to work." (Interview, July 2, 1985)

Courtesy of the Maxwell Museum of Anthropology.

Zuni polychrome olla with deer design, 1928. Arizona State Museum, Cat. No. E-1980.

"We paint the deer so that our husbands may have luck in hunting. . . . We like to have pictures of the deer in our houses like the white people have pictures of God." (Zuni potter quoted by Bunzel in *The Pueblo Potter,* 1929)

Photograph by Helga Teiwes. Courtesy of the Arizona State Museum.

Prayer to the Rainmakers

My fathers,
Your waters,
Your seeds,
Your riches,
Your power,
Your strong spirit,
All this you will grant us;
May my road be fulfilled,
May I grow old,
Even until I go with strong hands
grasping a bent stick,
Thus may I grow old.

(*Zuni Ritual Poetry,* 1932)

Bunzel saw herself as "but the mouthpiece" for the Zuni. She worked extensively with ritual texts because she felt that one should "structure an inquiry within a framework that is meaningful in the culture—in Zuni, first with a collection of drawings of masked dancers and later with a series of ritual texts." (*Chichicastenango,* 1952)

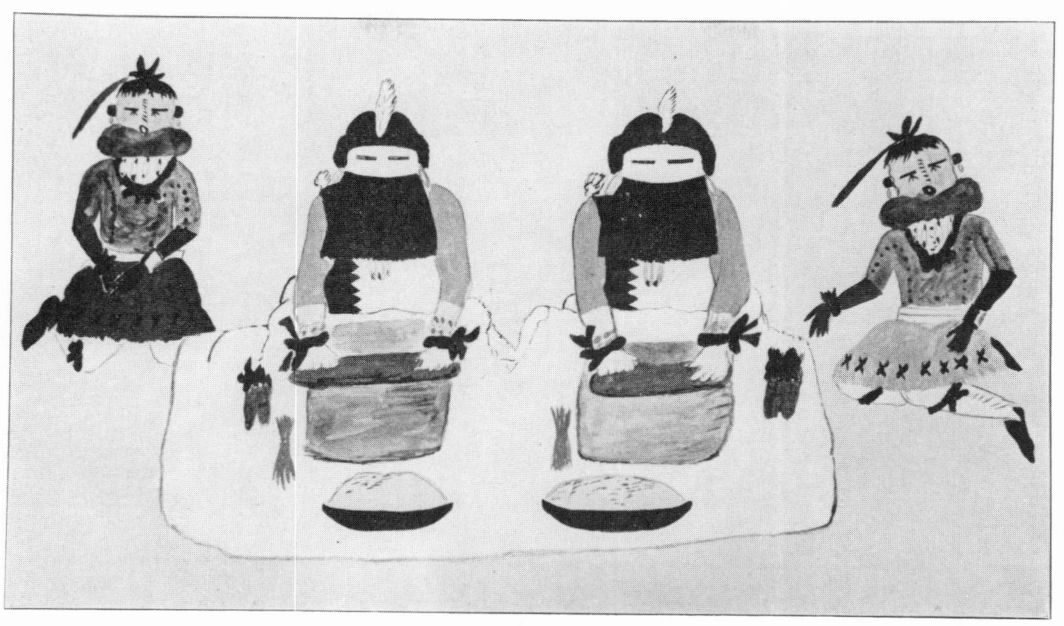

(*top*) Winter and Summer Dances: Katcina Corn Grinding (Plate 36). (*Zuni Katcinas*. 47th Annual Report of the Bureau of American Ethnology, 1932.)

(*bottom*) Dancing Katcinas: Winter Dances (Plate 46).

Courtesy of the National Anthropological Archives, Smithsonian Institution.

NAVAJO

Because of the difficulty of reaching their scattered hogans, few anthropologists worked among the Navajo before 1925. Traders such as Franc Newcomb were critically important in collecting Navajo materials and introducing women scholars to these now much-studied Athabascan people.

Wishing to have comparative southwestern materials, in 1923 Parsons encouraged another Boas student, Gladys Reichard, to study Navajo social organization. Reichard was followed by Katherine Spencer and Malcolm Collier in the 1930s and 1940s, and by Mary Shepardson and Blodwen Hammond in the 1960s. Although their perspectives differed, these women shared in common a desire to understand Navajo culture and society from the native point of view.

Gladys Reichard, 1950.

"She was so bright. Her mind worked so fast you couldn't keep up with it. She was fun to work for. She just assumed you had a brain." (Kate Peck Kent, Interview, September 4, 1985)

Courtesy of the Museum of Northern Arizona.

Gladys Reichard, 1893–1955

"I was trying to learn the reactions of individuals to culture." ("Another Look at the Navajo," ca. 1950)

One of the first women anthropologists to study the Navajo, Gladys Reichard began her thirty years of fieldwork in 1923. "I started the study of Navajo social structure by accident, the genealogical method being used by my sponsor, Elsie Clews Parsons." After three summers of fieldwork, Reichard "concluded that a study of structure is indispensable for any kind of social study, but that it is by no means enough for the understanding of behavior, attitude and motivation." She decided that ". . . religion was the integrating force of Navajo culture," and devoted the rest of her career to its study. ("Another Look at the Navajo," ca. 1950)

Like her mentors, Franz Boas and Pliny Earle Goddard, Reichard attempted to live the life of the people she studied. "I even had a 'bead,' a token that I was known to the Navajo deities who preside over lightning, snakes, and arrows. . . . It signifies that I have undergone a ritual which lasted five nights and days." ("I Personally," 1949) A thorough, patient ethnographer who felt most at home in the Southwest, "the quality of her relationship with the Navajo was such that for her fieldwork was never a lonely or tedious chore, isolating her from the main currents of her life, but rather a happy homecoming to people she valued as human beings and whose joys and problems she was able to understand and share." (Ruth Bunzel, "Gladys A. Reichard: A Tribute," 1955)

EDUCATION: B.A., Swarthmore College, 1919; M.A., 1920, Ph.D., 1925,anthropology, Columbia University.

FELLOWSHIPS AND AWARDS: Lucretia Mott Fellowship, 1920; Research Fellowship, Columbia University, 1922–23; Guggenheim Fellowship, 1926, to study at the University of Hamburg; Morrison Prize of the New York Academy of Sciences, 1932; Chicago Folklore Prize for work on Coeur d'Alene mythology, 1948.

RESEARCH: Wiyot linguistic research, studying grammar, 1922–23; fieldwork with the Navajo focused on social organization, religion, linguistics, and aesthetics, 1923 to 1955; Melanesian design through museum collections, 1926–27; Coeur d'Alene, folklore, 1938; spent summers based at Museum of Northern Arizona, 1940–55; Salish linguistics, 1954.

PROFESSIONAL ACTIVITIES: Elementary School Teacher, 1909–15; Instructor to Professor, Barnard College, 1923–55; wrote orthography of Navajo and organized Navajo Language School for BIA, 1934; Secretary, AES, 1924–26; President, AES, 1934–35; Executive Board, AES, 1924–44; Editor, *JAF,* 1940; Secretary AFS, 1924–36; Member of AAA Board, 1931, 1933; President, AAA, 1933–35; Executive Council Member, AAA, 1945–48; Director, 1946; Secretary, Linguistic Circle, 1946–47; Secretary, Section H, AAAS, 1945; Member Board of Trustees, Museum of Northern Arizona, 1950–55.

Columbia University anthropology picnic, ca. 1925. (*left to right*) Nels Nelson, Esther Goldfrank, Franz Boas, Gertrude Boas, Robert Lowie, Gladys Reichard, Pliny Earle Goddard, William Ogburn, Mrs. Nelson.

A familial atmosphere developed at Columbia University under Franz Boas's leadership. Reichard, like many other students, called him "Papa Franz."

Courtesy of the National Anthropological Archives, Smithsonian Institution.

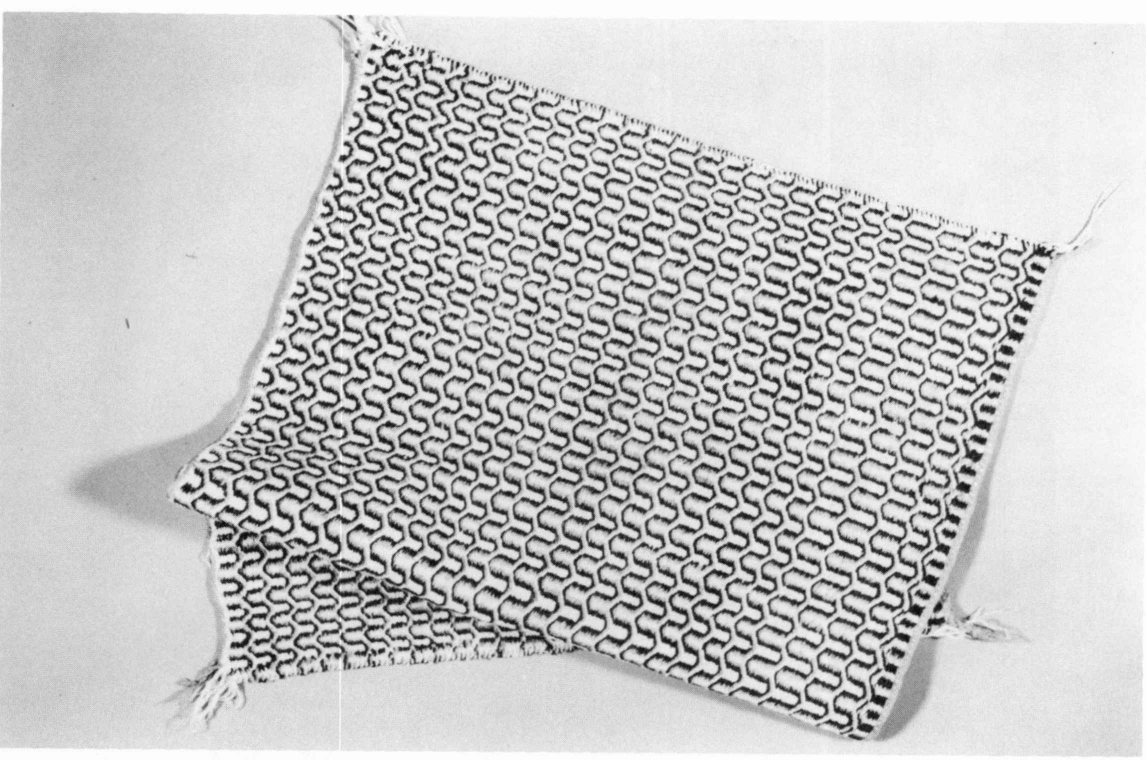

Saddle blanket made by Gladys Reichard in 1930 under the direction of Maria Antonia and Atlnaba.

Gladys Reichard "decided that learning to weave would be a way of developing the trust of the women. . . . By weaving, I could observe the daily round as a participant, rather than as a mere onlooker." (Another Look at the Navajo," ca. 1950)

Courtesy of Nathalie and Richard Woodbury. Photograph by Helga Teiwes. Courtesy of the Arizona State Museum.

Navajo Weavers, ca. 1960.

"The Navajo word for 'teach' is to 'show,' and that is exactly what they do. 'My grandmothers and sisters' showed me with unfailing patience and persistent good humor, each step in the long process of transforming wool from a sheep's back to the rug." (*Navajo Shepherd and Weaver,* 1936)

Courtesy of A.E. "Gene" Magee.

Adolph Bittany teaching at Navajo Language School, 1934.

Gladys Reichard and her translator, Adolph Bittany, taught Navajo school teachers to write Navajo for the first time in 1934. They believed that this would make the students' transition to English easier.

Photograph by Gladys Reichard. Courtesy of the Museum of Northern Arizona.

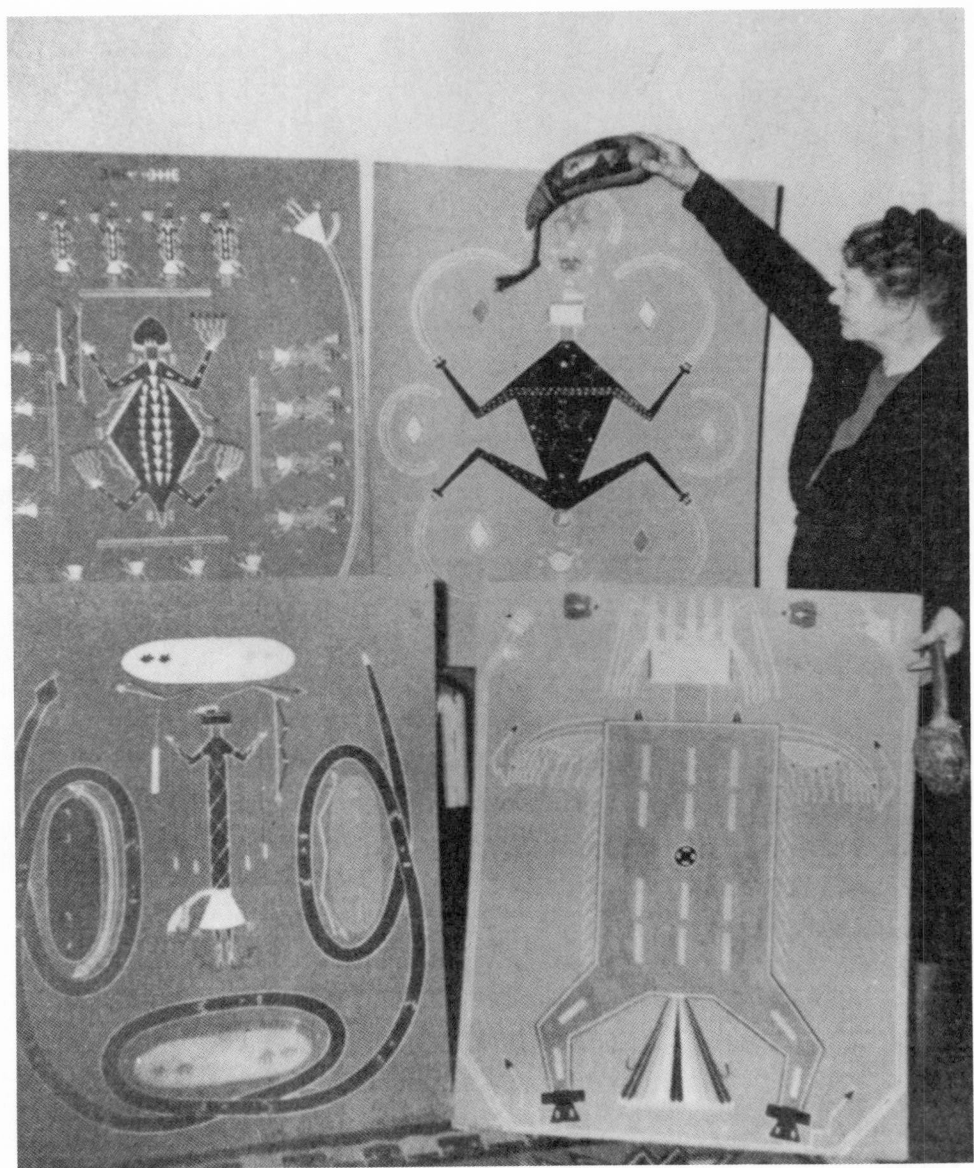

Franc Johnson Newcomb, showing a few of the sketches from her collection of sandpaintings.

"Little did I think, when I saw my first group of Navaho Indians standing near the Santa Fe depot in Gallup, New Mexico, that I would spend more than thirty years of my life among these people." (*Navaho Neighbors,* 1966)

Courtesy of the University of Oklahoma Press.

FRANC NEWCOMB, 1887–1970

"Navajos are people, not objects of study."
(Letter to Gladys Reichard, January 5, 1939)

Franc Johnson had been a BIA school teacher at Fort Defiance for two years when she married Arthur Newcomb and bought a trading post at Nava, New Mexico. Befriended by Hosteen Klah, a Nightway singer, she attended Navajo ceremonies. After a "friendly scolding" from Jessie Walter Fewkes "for not taking advantage of an ideal situation" (*Hosteen Klah,* 1964), Newcomb began memorizing the details of the Navajo's ephemeral sandpaintings. By 1948, when she sold her trading post, she had recorded more than 800 different sandpainting designs.

In 1932, Franc Newcomb met Gladys Reichard and they collaborated on *Sandpaintings of the Navajo Shooting Chant.* Newcomb, "the chronic collector," as she referred to herself, benefited from Reichard's writing skills and anthropological perspective. Newcomb later wrote several books on Navajo folklore on her own and collaborated with other anthropologists such as Leland Wyman.

EDUCATION: Diploma, Tomah High School, 1904; Certificate, teacher training, Sparta Normal School, Wisconsin, 1905.

FELLOWSHIPS AND AWARDS: Grant from Huckell family and Fred Harvey Co. to gather sandpaintings from Beadway, 1938–39; Woman of the Year, National League of American Pen Women, 1964; New Mexico Folklore Society Scroll of Honor, 1966.

RESEARCH: Navajo reservation, concentrating on religion and folklore, 1912–36.

PROFESSIONAL ACTIVITIES: School teacher in Wisconsin, 1905–09, on Menomini Reservation, 1911–12, on Navajo Reservation, 1912–14; trader on Navajo Reservation, 1914–36; professional writer and lecturer on Navajo history, legends and ceremonies, 1936–70; welfare activist; patron of New Mexico Museum, Albuquerque Little Theater; President of Albuquerque Women's Club; Member, Board of Directors, United Way; helped found several civic organizations; lobbyist for women's rights in New Mexico; poet.

Franc and Arthur Newcomb watching a Navajo weaver, ca. 1924.

As traders the Newcombs were interested in Navajo arts and crafts. While trading, Franc would often collect bits of information and stories.

Courtesy of the Museum of Northern Arizona.

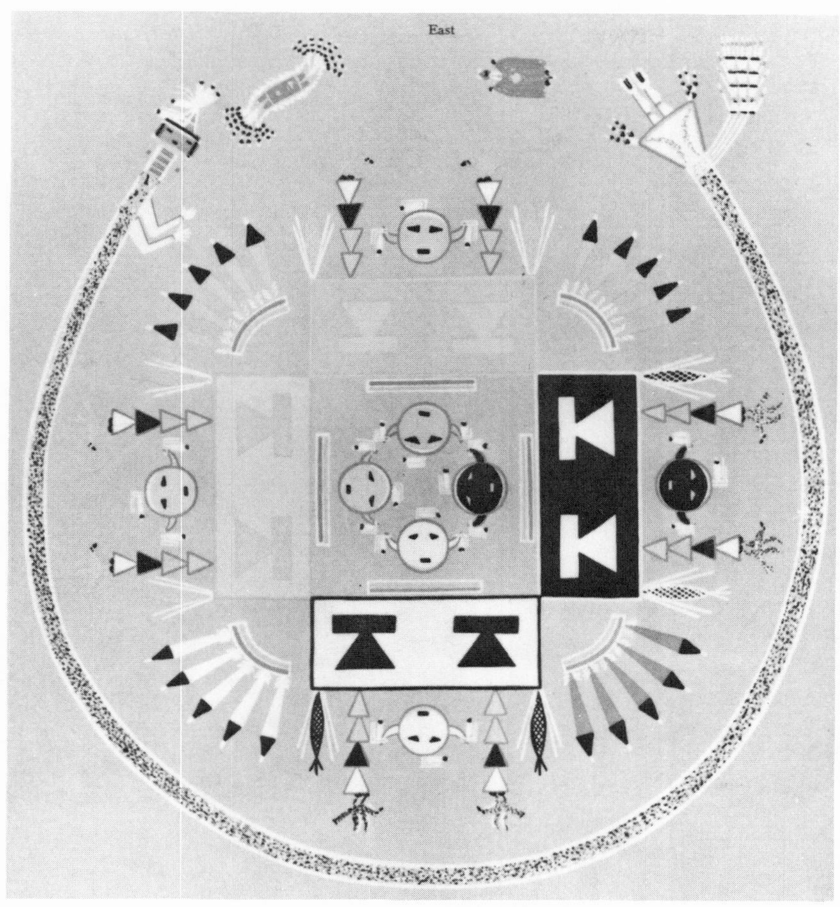

Cloud Houses from Male Shooting Chant. (*Sandpaintings of the Navajo Shooting Chant,* 1937)

Franc Newcomb and Gladys Reichard worked extensively together on books dealing with Navajo sandpaintings, the ephemeral designs used during curing ceremonies.

Courtesy of Dover Publications.

Katherine Spencer at Rainbow Bridge, Navajo Reservation, 1937.

"At each stage in my career, there was both the straight academic interest, and always an interest in applications." (Interview, September 3, 1985)

Courtesy of Katherine Spencer Halpern.

Katherine Spencer Halpern, 1913–

"In all cultures there are limitations and difficulties in the way of successful expression of human impulses and in the satisfaction of human needs." (*Mythology and Values: An Analysis of Navajo Chantway Myths,* 1957)

Katherine Spencer has combined social work and anthropology in a many faceted career. A graduate of the University of Chicago, Spencer received "generous encouragement and support" from Clyde Kluckhohn for her earliest work with the Navajo. As a member of Harvard University's Comparative Values Study she collected material for her book, *Mythology and Values: An Analysis of Navaho Chantway Myths* (1957) which "explored a portion of Navaho mythology to see what light it threw on the life view and values."

After World War II Spencer's research interests shifted to applied anthropology and mental health. In the mid 1960s, she studied physical and psychological handicaps in children and the Navajo attitude toward them. "I was interested in how social work students might come to know more about work with Indians." In addition, she tried to see "how Navajo parents could be brought more fully into active partnership with medical personnel." ("Impoverished Navajo Indians Are Stark Culture Contrast," 1965)

EDUCATION: B.A., chemistry, Vassar College, 1935; M.A., 1944, Ph.D., 1952, anthropology, University of Chicago. Additional course work in social work and mental health, University of Chicago, 1935–36 and Boston Psychoanalytic Institute, 1947–50.

FELLOWSHIPS AND AWARDS: SSRC Predoctoral Fellow, 1941–42; NIMH training grants for social work, 1962–69; USPHS, Indian Health Service grants, 1965, 1968, 1976; HEW grants, 1966–67; NIMH grants, 1967–68, 1976.

RESEARCH: Navajo kinship and social organization at Pueblo Alto, 1937; Community study—Matanuska Valley Resettlement Colony, Alaska, 1941–43; Navajo research with Clyde Kluckhohn, 1946–50; fieldwork on Navajo health and welfare problems, 1964–72.

PROFESSIONAL ACTIVITIES: Research Assistant, Harvard University, 1939–41; Case Consultant and Social Science Analyst, American Red Cross, 1942–46; Research Fellow, Harvard University, 1949–50; Consultant on several mental health projects for universities, federal agencies, the Navajo Tribe, and BIA, including training Navajo paraprofessionals and mental health aides, 1950–71; Associate Director, Community Health Project, Harvard University, 1953–57; Associate Professor and Professor, Boston University School of Social Work and Lecturer in Department of Anthropology, 1954–70; Research Associate, McLean Hospital, 1958–67; Research Associate, Harvard Medical School, 1960–66; advisory committees on social work and applied anthropology, 1962–76; Professor to Professor Emerita, Anthropology, American University, 1970–85; Researcher, Wheelwright Museum, 1979–85.

Doriane Woolley, Katherine Spencer, and friend at Cozy McSparron's Trading Post, Chinle, Arizona, in 1937.

With fellow student Malcolm Collier, Woolley and Spencer split a University of New Mexico fellowship to study with Kluckhohn. This opportunity had been arranged by University of Chicago anthropologist Fay-Cooper Cole. "It was," Halpern recalled, "really just an excuse to get there." (Interview, September 3, 1985)

Courtesy of Katherine Spencer Halpern.

Clyde Kluckhohn, 1905–1960.

Spencer's first trip to the Navajo reservation was as a student at the Chaco Canyon field school under the direction of Clyde Kluckhohn. "He became a more important person to me in my anthropological development than my professors at the University of Chicago. He was so encouraging to women students." (Interview, September 3, 1985)

Photograph by John Brock. Courtesy of the Peabody Museum of American Archaeology and Ethnology, Harvard University.

Navajo interpreter Willie (*left*) with Spencer's informants, his older relatives, near Chaco Canyon in 1937.

"Kluckhohn arranged for us to have an interpreter and we worked with Navajo clans in the Pueblo Alto area near Chaco Canyon. It was just a wonderful summer for the three of us." (Interview, September 3, 1985)

Courtesy of Katherine Spencer Halpern.

"East Mountain." Painting by Harrison Begay showing the Navajo origin myth, 1959. (*The Sacred Mountain of the Navajo,* 1967)

Spencer used mythology and folklore to study Navajo values and world view. She intended to work in applied anthropology and social work, but her interest in folklore and mythology was encouraged when she was Kluckhohn's research assistant.

Courtesy of the Museum of Northern Arizona Press.

Malcolm Collier at the Chaco Canyon Field School, Summer, 1937.

"I suppose whatever course one follows in fieldwork, one might always have the feeling that another would be more fruitful." (Letter to Donald Collier, November 5, 1938)

Courtesy of Katherine Spencer Halpern.

Malcolm Collier, 1908–1983

"I shall not like leaving Navajo Mountain. I am very attached to the country and the people . . . and feel very much at home." (Letter to Donald Collier, December 13, 1938)

While attending a summer seminar and traveling in Mexico with her sister Sarah and Sarah's husband, René d'Harnoncourt, Malcolm Carr became so interested in Mexico's people and its past, that René suggested she go to graduate school and study anthropology. In 1936, she enrolled in the Department of Anthropology at the University of Chicago and later married fellow graduate student, Donald Collier. While attending the 1937 Chaco Canyon Summer Field School, she, Katherine Spencer, and Doriane Woolley persuaded Clyde Kluckhohn to allow them to study kinship and clans in the Navajo community of Pueblo Alto. Malcolm returned for further research in 1938–39 at Klagetoh and Navajo Mountain, where she gathered data on local organization. This research was the basis of her disseration, valuable both to David Aberle in his work on Navajo kinship and to Mary Shepardson and Blodwen Hammond for their comparative restudy of the same community twenty-five years later.

Recognizing that the social sciences were unrepresented or misrepresented in secondary schooling, Collier originated, organized, and directed the Anthropology Curriculum Study Project of the American Anthropological Association. Her work on this project between 1961 and 1972 was influential in bringing anthropology to 265 school teachers and more than 40,000 students and laid the foundation for the Council on Anthropology and Education.

EDUCATION: B.A., Wellesley, 1930, French; piano study, Vienna, Austria, 1930–31; attends summer seminars, Mexico, 1932, anthropology; graduate study in anthropology, University of Chicago, 1936–38; University of New Mexico field school, 1937; Ph.D., Chicago, 1951.

FELLOWSHIPS AND AWARDS: Research Assistant, U.S. Indian Service, 1938–39; 10 NSF grants supporting the Anthropology Curriculum Study Project, 1962–1972.

RESEARCH: Navajo kinship and social organization at Pueblo Alto, Klagetoh and Navajo Mountain, 1937–39.

PROFESSIONAL ACTIVITIES: Lecturer, Downtown College of the University of Chicago; Assistant Editor, *American Anthropologist;* Assistant Editor, *Current Anthropology;* Assistant organizer, Darwin Centennial, University of Chicago, 1958–59; Research Associate, Department of Anthropology, University of Chicago, 1960–70; Director, Anthropology Curriculum Study Project, 1961–1972.

Malcolm Collier with Francis Clark, son of her interpreter Madge Clark, Klagetoh, summer of 1939.

"I still seem able to get more information and insight by a rather informal type of work than any other way." (Letter to Donald Collier, November 5, 1938)

Courtesy of Donald Collier.

THE CLAN

The names of 39 clans were mentioned at one time or another by informants. Of these, 31 are represented in the genealogies. In the following table[24] the names of clans not represented in the genealogies are given in parentheses.

Clan Name	*Translation*	*Membership at Pueblo Alto*
1. ta?ne·szahni·	Pitched Hogans	78
2. ʒiłƛ̇ahni·	Canyon in the Mountain	14
3. ho?né·γani·	Place of Going Around, or Place Stuck On	2
4. tó?axani	Live Close to Water	10
5. naho·bani	See Gray Long Distance	14
6. haškąhaʒohó	Piles of Yucca Fruit	1
7. ho·γąłání	Many Hogans	16
9. biťahni·	Folded Arms, or Under His Blanket People	51
10. tócohni·	Big Water	8
12. hašƛ̇išni·	Mud	45
13. naneštéži	Zuni	49
14. ƛ̇ízáłání	Many Goats	5
(15. kinłičí·ní·	Red House)	
16. ƛ̇á·ščí?í	Underside Red	10
17. cina·ǯini	Something Black Coming Down Hill	4
18. cenahabiłni·	Close to Rock	21
(19. desčí·ni	Red Streak)	
20. táči·ni·	See Something Red Under	50
22. ki·ya?â·ni·	Standing House	93
23. bíta·ni	Branching Leaves	2
24. tó?oxe·λí·ni·	Where Waters Come Together	51
25. na·kaidiné?é	Mexican	27
(26. ċeké?é)		
27. noda?í	Ute	11
28. cinzakadiné	Cedars Standing by Themselves	8
29. tódíčí·?ni·	Bitter Water	53
(30. bį·hbitó	Deer Spring)	
32. ?ášį·hí	Salt	127
33. ma?i·de·šgi·zni	Jemez	2
(34. dibéłižiní	Black Sheep)	
36. tábą·há	Edge of Water; or Lives Near Lake	6
37. halcô·	Yellow in the Distance	1
(38. cénžokin	Black House)	
39. ċahiskidni·	Sagebrush Hill	3
40. ƛ̇ógí	Zia	1
43. tóba·žná?áží	Two Persons Went After Water	1
46. na·šaší	Enemy Bear	1
(47. tąži·	Turkey People)	
a. te?ati·n	Trail to the Garden	111
dinedobehazan		4
Pueblo people		8
	Total	888

List of Navajo clans from "Navajo Clans and Marriage at Pueblo Alto" (*American Anthropologist,* 1939).

In 1937, Carr, Spencer, and Woolley collected information on genealogies and clan affiliations "with the hope that a regional study of the Navaho clan and its relationship to marriage might be useful as a matter of record and for comparison with other areas." ("Navajo Clans and Marriage at Pueblo Alto" 1939)

Courtesy of the American Anthropological Association. Photograph by Helga Teiwes. Courtesy of the Arizona State Museum.

(*facing page, bottom*) Traditional Navajo wedding of Annie Dodge and George Wauneka (2nd and 3rd from left), ca. 1930.

In 1938, Malcolm Carr traveled to the isolated community of Navajo Mountain. Here she "made one of the few detailed studies of Navajo social organization to be found in the anthropological literature. Her specific data could be used for comparison with the specific data we would accumulate for a study of persistence and change after a span of twenty-five years." (Mary Shepardson and Blowden Hammond, *The Navajo Mountain Community,* 1970).

Photograph by Milton Snow. Courtesy of the BIA, Milton Snow Collection, Navajo Tribal Museum, Window Rock, Arizona.

Mary Shepardson and Blodwen Hammond leaving for the Navajo Reservation, 1960.

"They were surprised and happy to see their *Sáani,* 'old ladies' (Blodwen and me), and our honesty was quickly established." (*Fieldwork among the Navajo,* 1986)

Courtesy of Mary Shepardson.

MARY SHEPARDSON, 1906–

"I have tried to evaluate problems within a broad framework of inquiry, reading, and participation as an observer." (*Navajo Ways in Government,* 1963)

Mary Shepardson came to anthropology late in life. Like Katherine Spencer, she was "welcomed with kindness and enthusiasm into an exciting collective enterprise—the study of human behavior" by Clyde Kluckhohn. Shepardson's research focused on culture change and the effects of Anglo-American ideas and values on Navajo political organization. "My aim is to present with understanding the conflicting opinions and interests which make up developing political process among the Navajo Indians." (*Navajo Ways in Government,* 1963)

Shepardson was interested in community studies and with her colleague, Blodwen Hammond, she worked at Navajo Mountain from 1960 to 1962, studying "basic societal functions" and the persistence of traditional patterns. They chose "the scenic area of Navajo Mountain . . . for its stunning beauty," its isolation, and because "Malcolm Carr Collier had made one of the few detailed studies of Navajo social organization" here in 1938. (*The Navajo Mountain Community,* 1970) Shepardson also assisted Navajo leader Irene Stewart in writing her autobiography, *A Voice in Her Tribe* (1980).

EDUCATION: Sorbonne, certificate in civilisation française, 1927; A.B., Stanford University, 1928; M.A., anthropology, Stanford University, 1956; Ph.D., anthropology, University of California–Berkeley, 1960.

FELLOWSHIPS AND AWARDS: NSF, 1960–61; NIMH grants, 1962–67; APS Fellow, 1969; NIMH grant, 1971–73.

RESEARCH: Fieldwork on Navajo Reservation on political and social organization, 1954–67, 1969, 1971–73, 1975; study of ethnic enclaves, Bonin Islands.

PROFESSIONAL ACTIVITIES: Research Associate, University of Chicago, 1961–67; Lecturer and Associate Professor, 1967–73, Professor Emerita, 1973–86, San Francisco State College; Consultant, Bureau of Reclamation, 1975; Visiting Professor, Mills College and Stanford University, 1977–78; Editor, *Southwest Anthropology Association Newsletter,* 1969–70.

Irene Stewart, 1980.

Shepardson helped Irene Stewart write the story of her life. "My first interview with Irene Stewart in 1955 marked the beginning of an acquaintanceship which . . . grew into a deep and enduring friendship between two women across the cultural divide." (*A Voice in Her Tribe,* 1980)

From *A Voice in Her Tribe,* 1980. Courtesy of Ballena Press.

(*facing page, top*) Mary Shepardson and Jackson Greymountain, Navajo Mountain, 1961.

"Whenever I see the road sign YOU ARE ENTERING THE NAVAJO INDIAN RESERVATION I feel a lift of the heart." (*Fieldwork among the Navajo,* 1986)

Courtesy of Mary Shepardson.

(*facing page, bottom*) Navajo Tribal Council, ca. 1960.
With Irene Stewart, Shepardson "attended meetings, visited Chapters in many communities, observed the Tribal Council in session at Window Rock" to learn about Navajo political processes. Irene "acted as guide, interpreter, and friend." (*A Voice in Her Tribe,* 1980)

Courtesy of the Arizona State Museum.

Papago and Yaqui

The desert-dwelling Papago (Tohono O'Odham) were frequently visited but rarely studied prior to 1930. The harsh environment and their isolation in small villages enabled these Piman peoples to maintain their traditions despite several centuries of contact with Hispanics and Anglos.

Boas's interest in salvage ethnography and his "sympathy with women's ambitions," resulted in Ruth Underhill making, in 1931, the first of many cross-country drives to work among the Papago. Along with Frances Densmore's pioneering 1929 study of Papago music, Underhill's publications on Papago culture and society laid the groundwork for other ethnographers such as Rosamond Spicer.

Until 1887, the Yaqui of northwestern Mexico resisted attempts to bring them and their territory into the hacienda land system. Following military occupation by Diaz's troops, thousands of Yaqui emigrated to southern Arizona. By 1940, several anthropologists at the University of Arizona were studying and assisting these proud and scattered survivors who were attempting to rebuild their Sonoran communities.

With their friend and associate Muriel Painter, Rosamond and Edward Spicer devoted their careers to documenting Yaqui history and problems of culture change, and working to preserve and present the complex ceremonials so central to Yaqui identity and worldview.

Ruth Underhill, 1946.

"Boas and Benedict opened a door through which a light shined on me." (Interview, *Ruth Murray Underhill: Friend of the Desert People,* 1985)

Photograph by Laura Gilpin, copyright 1981. Courtesy of Laura Gilpin Collection, Amon Carter Museum.

Ruth Underhill, 1883–1984

"I was to learn it is the land that possesses the people. Its influence, in time, shapes their bodies, their language, even, a little, their religion." (*Papago Woman,* 1979)

After a twenty-year career in social work, Ruth Underhill wanted "to know more about PEOPLE" and enrolled at Columbia University in 1930 to study anthropology. Ruth Benedict encouraged her to study culture as it is expressed in individual personalities. Underhill's first weeks among the Tohono O'Odham "were spent almost entirely with women," the most important of whom was Chona. Chona's story, *Autobiography of a Papago Woman* (1936), was the first published life history of a Southwestern Indian woman. Underhill returned repeatedly to the "hard-working but poetic" Papago who came to value her and her efforts "to capture the spirit of their people." (*Papago Woman,* 1979)

Underhill's fifty-year career in anthropology included thirteen years traveling to the reservations of the Southwest as a consultant for the Bureau of Indian Affairs. In this capacity, she wrote study books for Indian children as well as several important books and pamphlets interpreting the Indians of the Southwest to the general public.

EDUCATION: B.A., English, Vassar College, 1905; Ph.D., anthropology, Columbia University, 1935. Courses at London School of Economics and University of Munich, 1908–09.

FELLOWSHIPS AND AWARDS: Columbia Humanities Council, 1933–1934, to study Papago and Mohave; Bloch Community Scholarship, 1962; Citation for public service, Colorado Women's College, 1963; LL.D., University of Denver, 1962; D.Sc., University of Colorado, 1965; Tohono O'Odham honors, 1979.

RESEARCH: Ethnographic research with Tohono O'Odham and Mohave, 1931–33; fieldwork for BIA with various Indian groups, 1934–49.

PROFESSIONAL ACTIVITIES: Case worker, Massachusetts Society for the Prevention of Cruelty to Children, 1905–08; Social worker, Charity Organization Society, 1913–14; American Red Cross, 1915–18; Administrator, Italian Orphanage, Italy, 1918–20; Assistant in anthropology at Barnard College, 1930–34; AAA Council, 1931–48; Soil Conservationist, U.S. Department of Agriculture, 1933–34; Anthropologist, BIA, 1934–49; Anthropology Society of Washington Board, 1941–42; Professor, University of Denver, 1948–52; Professor Emerita and Distinguished Lecturer at various colleges, 1952–84; Lecturer on Indians for series of 30 educational television programs; Interviewer of Indians for radio series; Board Member, International House of Denver, 1958–84; President, AES, 1961–62.

Chona making a basket, 1931.

"Chona was making a basket. She sat on the floor as proper Indian women sit, with legs bent to the side, not spread in the man's style. Before her was a bunch of willow withes and a dishpan of water for soaking them. She was splitting one wand between her teeth, and now she brandished it in a hand as brown and rough-skinned as a tree branch with its twigs." (*Papago Woman,* 1979)

Photograph by Ruth Underhill. Courtesy of the Denver Museum of Natural History.

(*facing page, top*) Ruth Underhill interviewing a Tohono O'Odham man, ca. 1931.

"I could have spent a life among the Papago, but in those days we did not get grants easily, as students do now." (*Papago Woman,* 1979)

Courtesy of the Denver Museum of Natural History.

(*facing page, bottom*) Tohono O'Odham Parade honoring Ruth Underhill, 1979.

"We, the People of the Crimson Evening, the O'Odham, recognize your efforts and your talents in preserving and capturing the spirit of our people, for this generation and for future generations to come." ("To Ruth Murray Underhill," Julie Pierson, 1979)

Photograph by Helga Teiwes. Courtesy of the Arizona State Museum.

DR. RUTH UNDERHILL
GRAND★MARSHALL
PAPAGO RODEO PARADE

Rosamond Spicer returning from field session, 1942.

"The person who took the picture said I was dressed as she thought an anthropologist ought to be!" (Interview, August 20, 1985)

Courtesy of Rosamond Spicer.

Rosamond Spicer, 1913–

"You do anthropology no matter what you do."
(Interview, August 20, 1985)

Rosamond Brown went to the University of Chicago intending to become an Egyptologist. Drawn into cultural anthropology and "studying people rather than digging in the ground," she met and married fellow student Edward Spicer. In 1936, they spent their honeymoon with the Yaqui at Pascua Village. Roz and Ned Spicer "worked together whatever it was." (Interview, August 20, 1985) Their community studies made them one of the most famous husband and wife teams in southwestern anthropology.

During World War II, Spicer worked with the Papago on the Indian Education and Research Project and, with Alice Joseph and Jane Chesky, produced *The Desert People* (1949). Thereafter, her energies and attention shifted from community studies to civic activities. Through her work with dance, with civil rights, with the Tucson Community School, and with the Old Ft. Lowell Neighborhood Association, she has "made a difference in the community life in Arizona." (Interview, August 20, 1985)

EDUCATION: B.A., anthropology, Northwestern University, 1934; M.A., anthropology, University of Chicago, 1939.

FELLOWSHIPS AND AWARDS: several grants with Edward B. Spicer to study Yaqui, 1940–42; Wenner-Gren Foundation Grant for archival management, 1984–86.

RESEARCH: Yaqui ethnographic research and community studies at Pascua and Potam, 1936–37, 1940–42; Black youths in New Orleans, 1938–39; Papago, social and political organization, community studies, 1942–44; Japanese-Americans in Relocation Centers, 1943–45; Seri linguistics, 1950.

PROFESSIONAL ACTIVITIES: Painter, 1930–32; Volunteer assistant, University of Pennsylvania Museum, 1933–34; Student assistant, University of Chicago, 1934–36; Analyst, American Youth Commission, 1938–39; Assistant, University of Chicago field school, 1938–39; Volunteer, Arizona State Museum, 1939–40; Social Science Analyst, Research on Indian Education, BIA–University of Chicago Committee on Human Development, 1942–43; Social Science Analyst, Bureau of Sociological Research, BIA, 1943–44; Information Specialist, War Relocation Authority, 1944–46; Executive Secretary, Arizona Council for Civic Unity, 1948–50; President and Trustee, Tucson Community School, 1948–78; Secretary, Tucson Urban League, 1949; Volunteer, Cornell Field School in Applied Anthropology, 1948–50; Assistant Editor, *American Anthropologist,* 1960–63; Member, Pima County Fort Lowell Historic District Board, 1973–76; Consultant, Arizona Humanities Council, 1981.

Rosamond, Barry, and Edward Spicer at Old Pascua Village (Yaqui Reservation), April 13, 1941.

"I have always felt that what I was interested in I would go do, and it didn't matter whether I was a man or a woman." (Interview, August 20, 1985)

Courtesy of Rosamond Spicer.

Yaqui George Garcia playing flute, Old Pascua Village, 1968.

Garcia worked with the Spicers for many years.

Dr. R.W. Payne Collection. Courtesy of the Arizona State Museum.

Rosamond Spicer with son Robert B. "Barry" Spicer and Juana de Amarillas at Topawa (Papago Reservation), 1943.

"I certainly think that having my child with me was helpful there. They recognized that I was a normal kind of person and they appreciated the fact that I would bring a child out there to be with them. They simply trusted me more." (Interview, August 20, 1985)

Courtesy of Rosamond Spicer.

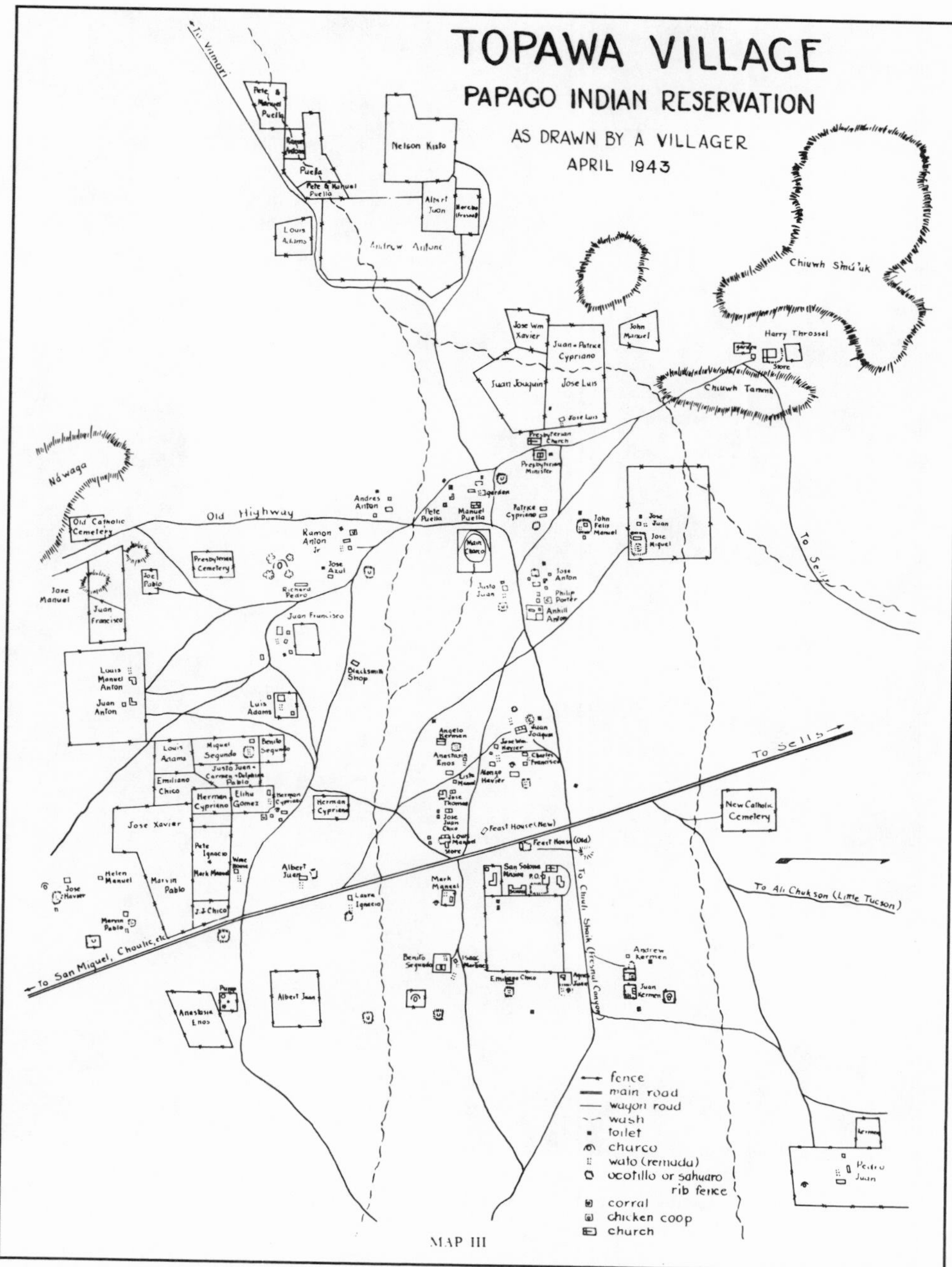

Map of Topawa Village, Papago Reservation drawn by Roz Spicer for *The Desert People*, 1949.

While working on the Indian Education and Research Project, Spicer conducted a community study of four villages in the Topawa district.

Courtesy of the University of Chicago Press.

Muriel Painter at New Pascua Village (Yaqui Reservation) during Easter Ceremony, 1968.

"What would I do without the Yaquis? I get much more out of it than I put in." (Interview, *Tucson Daily Citizen,* April 10, 1963)

Courtesy of Rosamond Spicer.

Muriel Painter, 1892–1975

"There is chance for so many innocent blunders when working with another culture." ("Final Report to Tucson Festival Society," 1952)

Muriel Painter began her work with the Yaqui in 1939, encouraged by her friend the famous social anthropologist, Bronislaw Malinowski. Although she never held a professional position, her exhaustive documentation of Yaqui life and her extensive oral histories established her as a regionally respected anthropologist.

Ms. Painter was an activist with great concern for the well-being of her Yaqui friends. She consciously promoted the Yaqui Easter ceremonies and founded the San Xavier Fiesta in 1951. "I wrote *Faith, Flowers, and Fiestas* (1962) and *A Yaqui Easter* (1970) to help visitors understand the ceremonies." (Interview, *Tucson Daily Citizen,* April 10, 1963) She served as chairman of the Committee for Pascua Community Housing and worked tirelessly on the Yaqui's behalf.

EDUCATION: B.A., Wellesley College, 1916; graduate studies in anthropology at University of Arizona, 1940; University of Mexico, 1943; Harvard University, 1946.

RESEARCH: Yaqui, concentrating on Easter ceremonies and life histories, 1939–75; Papago, religious ceremonies and Papago Indian Fair and Rodeo, 1946–57.

PROFESSIONAL ACTIVITIES: Social caseworker in New York City, Boston, and Minneapolis, 1916–31; Chairperson, Chamber of Commerce Yaqui Easter Committee, 1942–51; Freelance journalist, Tucson newspapers, 1943–45; Chairperson, Committee to the Pascua Yaqui Assocation, 1962–69; Chairperson, San Xavier Ceremony of the Tucson Festival Society, 1952–56; Research Associate, Arizona State Museum, 1944–75.

Pascola and Deer Dancer at a Yaqui Fiesta.

"The Deer dances with each Pascola in turn, but only when the Pascolas dance to the music of their flute-drummer." (*Faith, Flowers and Fiestas,* 1962)

Courtesy of the Arizona State Museum and the University of Arizona Press.

Yaqui Dance equipment.

Nowhere does the blending of old and new appear more clearly than in Yaqui religion. "Dancing is as much a religious devotion among the Yaqui as is praying or singing." (Spicer, *The Yaqui,* 1980)

(*left to right*) Yaqui Deer Dancer disc rattles, "Sonasum," used by Pascola dancers. Collected by Edward and Rosamond Spicer, 1940. Arizona State Museum, Cat. No. E-526, E-1253.

Yaqui flute used to accompany Pascola Dancer. Collected by Edward H. Spicer, ca. 1940. Arizona State Museum, Cat. No. E-1380.

Yaqui Deer Dancer's headdress. Collected by Muriel Painter, before 1970. Arizona State Museum, Cat. No. AT-75-22-73.

Yaqui Pascola mask. Collected by Edward and Rosamond Spicer, ca. 1940. Arizona State Museum, Cat. No. E-234.

Photograph by Helga Teiwes. Courtesy of the Arizona State Museum.

"Little Angels" by Micaela Espinosa.

"Children dressed as angels, with flower crowns, are part of the church group during Lent. They carry switches to guard the altar and the holy figures from the Fariseos." (*Faith, Flowers and Fiestas*, 1962.)

Courtesy of the University of Arizona Press. Photographs by Helga Teiwes. Courtesy of the Arizona State Museum.

Pascua Yaqui Development Project Adobes, 1966–67.

"The important thing is not to impose a way of life on the Yaquis which is inconsistent with the ways of their culture." ("Yaqui Housing Diary," June 3, 1963)

Photograph by Helga Teiwes. Courtesy of the Arizona State Museum.

3 • Interpreting the Native American

In the past century, southwestern anthropology has been characterized not only by an increasing concern with cultural diversity but by its interpretive diversity. The development of American anthropology meant not only institutional diversification and theoretical and methodological specialization but the establishment of subdisciplines. By the late 1920s, the non-specific interest in cultural diversity and the scope of human variation and in doing total ethnographies began to yield to more problem-oriented fieldwork: How does an artist think about her work? What is adolescence like in different societies? How do individuals perceive and represent their lives? Not surprisingly much women's research concentrated on those aspects of culture regarded as "expressive" or "feminine" and women generally worked in those subdisciplines which had low status or low priority in the discipline. Even when women did specialize and excel in a "masculine" subfield such as archaeology, few held academic positions.

Prior to World War II, much anthropology was practiced in non- or quasi-academic contexts and in the Southwest, much of that was done by women. While their male colleagues worked at being more "scientific" and at professionalizing and institutionalizing the discipline, a majority of women anthropologists dedicated themselves to translating the findings of anthropological research and the complexities of southwestern Native American cultures to the general public. Although important and invaluable, such modes of anthropological discourse as museum pamphlets and exhibits, children's books, novels and photographic essays have been devalued and ignored. Obviously, there is a certain amount of circularity in this situation and it is impossible to say whether women worked in certain subfields and produced the type of discourse they did because those areas were regarded as marginal or in some sense suited to women *or* that those subfields and modes of writing were marginalized and devalued because they were dominated by women.

Folklore and Ethnomusicology

Beginning with the pioneering efforts of Matilda Coxe Stevenson, Natalie Curtis, and Frances Densmore at the turn of the century, women have made notable contributions to those subfields of anthropology such as folklore and ethnomusicology that study the "expressive" domains of Native American cultures. This interest reflected the areas stressed in the traditional Victorian and Edwardian education for middle class women. Because such studies were regarded as less important and "unscientific," they were often left to women and deemed "feminine." Given his interest in and encouragement both of these domains of culture and of women students, Boas was frequently criticized by his colleagues in Cambridge and Washington.

Frances Densmore wearing dress worn when giving lecture on Indian Music at Chicago Art Institute, February 21, 1899.

"I heard an Indian drum when I was very, very young. I have heard it in strange places, in the dawn and at midnight, with its mysterious throb." (Quoted in Charles Hofmann, *Frances Densmore and American Indian Music,* 1968)

Photograph by Phillips, Red Wing, Minnesota. Courtesy of the National Anthropological Archives, Smithsonian Institution.

Frances Densmore, 1867–1957

"My work has been to preserve the past, record observations in the present, and open the way for the work of others in the future." ("The Study of Indian Music," 1942)

Densmore's success in lecturing on Native American music led her to fieldwork with the Chippewa in 1905 and the Sioux in 1906. While her early work dealt with the beauty of the lyrics, she soon realized the inadequacy of transcriptions alone for "nothing is lost so irrevocably as the sound of a song" (*Chippewa Music,* 1910). With a borrowed phonograph she returned to the White Mountain Reservation in 1907 and persuaded Big Bear to record 12 cylinders.

Densmore became and remains the most prolific collector of Native American music: she recorded more than 3,350 Native American songs by 1940. She worked with seventy-six groups from British Columbia to Florida, including the Papago, Yuma, Yaqui, Cocopa, Acoma, Isleta, Cochiti, and Zuni in the Southwest. "The Indians used songs as a means for accomplishing definite results. Singing was not a trivial matter." (*The American Indians and Their Music,* 1936)

EDUCATION: Musical training in piano, organ, and harmony, Oberlin Conservatory of Music, 1884–86; studied piano with Carl Baermann and counterpoint with John K. Paine, Harvard University, 1899–1890; M.A., music, Oberlin College, 1924.

FELLOWSHIPS AND AWARDS: Yearly funds from Smithsonian Institution for research, 1907–40; NRC grant, 1932–33; Southwest Museum Grant, 1935–37; University of Michigan Scholarship, 1945; Citation, Minnesota Historical Society, 1954; Award of National Association of American Composers, 1940–41; LL.D., MacAlaster College, 1950.

RESEARCH: Beginning in 1901 spends summers on Chippewa reservation; ethnomusicological research with 76 groups in Northwest Coast, Plains, and Southwest, including Papago (1920), Yuman and Yaqui (1922), Cocopa, and Acoma, Isleta, Cochiti, Zuni Pueblos. Between 1901 and 1940, makes over 3,350 sound recordings.

PROFESSIONAL ACTIVITIES: Piano teacher and lecturer on Wagnerian Music, 1893; Lecturer on American Indian Music, 1895–1950; Field Collaborator, BAE, Smithsonian Institution, 1907–57; AAA Council 1930–41; Consultant, National Archives, 1941–43; Consultant, Densmore Collection of Indian Music, Library of Congress, 1948–51; Researcher, Hill Reference Library, 1940; Executive Council, Society of Women Geographers, 1933–42; Associate, Southwest Museum, 1950–57.

2

Ramon Smith playing flute in Juan Ortega's yard, October 24, 1966.

In 1920, Frances Densmore recorded over 100 Tohono O'Odham songs for her pioneering study of Papago music. In addition to the songs, she recorded the stories connected with them such as the "Story of the Origin of the Flute," presented in extended form in *Papago Music* (1929).

Photograph by Helga Teiwes. Courtesy of the Arizona State Museum.

(*facing page, top*) Alice Cunningham Fletcher, ca. 1890, Chairperson of the managing board of the School of American Archaeology, 1907–1912.

"If Miss Fletcher had been less gracious in her response it is probable that I would not have taken up the study of Indian music." ("The Study of Indian Music," 1942)

Courtesy of the National Anthropological Archives, Smithsonian Institution.

(*facing page, bottom*) Frances Densmore with Big Bear, Sioux, White Mountain Reservation, interpreting his songs, 1914.

"The Indian does not sing of trials and tribulations, nor how he feels, but sings about the beautiful things in nature that lift him above the trials of life. He sings about the sky, and the winds and the clouds that sweep across it." (1927 lecture quoted in Hoffmann, "Frances Densmore and the Music of the American Indian," 1946)

Courtesy of the National Anthropological Archives, Smithsonian Institution.

Natalie Curtis Burlin with Pueblo friend, Dionicio, on the patio of the Palace of the Governors, Santa Fe, New Mexico, 1917.

"For truly we white people have here little to teach and much to learn." ("The Perpetuating of Indian Art," 1913)

Courtesy of the Museum of New Mexico.

NATALIE CURTIS BURLIN, 1875–1921

"The song of the southwestern Indian is the voice of the American desert. It is outlined on the vast silence as the clear-cut mountain line is traced upon the rainless sky." (*Songs of Ancient America,* 1905)

Natalie Curtis planned a career as a concert pianist and pursued her musical education in both America and Europe. While visiting her brother in Arizona after her return to America, she became interested in Indian music and in 1900 began the "self-appointed task of reverently recording" native songs. As she later recalled, "the voice sang on and I turned to seek it." ("Two Pueblo Indian Grinding Songs," 1904) She was, however, advised to keep her work secret since native songs and languages were forbidden in government schools. Enabled by family friendship, Curtis took her plea for Native American "cultural and spiritual" rights to President Roosevelt, whom she persuaded not only to lift the assimilationist ban prohibiting Indian music and language but also to enact policy to preserve and encourage Indian music, art, and poetry.

Curtis's sensitive and forward-looking scholarship was epitomized in *The Indians' Book* in which both title and prefatory note announce "The Indians are the authors of this volume." This collection of 200 songs from 18 tribes was so successful that Curtis received an urgent request to similarly record Afro-American music, which occupied the next decade of her life. Here, as with Native American music, she was indefatigable not only in meticulously recording "the spiritual life of a race," but in lecturing and writing to white America about the indigenous cultural heritage that it was ignoring if not destroying. When she was struck by a car in Paris in October, 1921, she had just delivered an address before the International Congress on the History of Art. At the time of her death she was planning to return to the study of Indian music and looking forward to a revision of *The Indians' Book*.

EDUCATION: Studied piano with Arthur Friedheim at the National Conservatory of Music; studied piano with Busoni in Berlin, Alfred Giraudet in Paris, Wolf in Bonn, and Julius Kniese at the Wagner-Schule in Bayreuth.

RESEARCH: Recorded the music and folklore of eighteen tribes, mainly Southwest, concentrating on Pueblo, 1900ff.; recorded Afro-American and African music, 1910–1915 under the auspices of the Hampton Normal and Agricultural Institute, Norfolk, Virginia.

PROFESSIONAL ACTIVITIES: Persuaded President Theodore Roosevelt to remove assimilationist ban prohibiting the singing of native songs; founded Music School Settlement for Colored People in Harlem, 1911; organized Carnegie Hall concert by Negro musicians, 1914; lectured frequently to scholarly, popular, and political audiences on Indian and Afro-American music; Executive Committee, Department of Ethnology of the Brooklyn Institute of Arts and Sciences; Member, American Folklore Society; Member, American Indian Association; Member, Santa Fe Society of the Archaeological Institute.

THE INDIANS' BOOK

AN OFFERING BY THE AMERICAN INDIANS OF INDIAN LORE, MUSICAL AND NARRATIVE, TO FORM A RECORD OF THE SONGS AND LEGENDS OF THEIR RACE

RECORDED AND EDITED BY

NATALIE CURTIS

ILLUSTRATIONS FROM PHOTOGRAPHS AND FROM ORIGINAL DRAWINGS BY INDIANS

NEW YORK AND LONDON
HARPER AND BROTHERS PUBLISHERS

Cover, *The Indians' Book.*

"My one desire has been to let the Indian songs be heard as the Indians themselves sing them." (*Songs of Ancient America,* 1905)

Courtesy of Harper and Brothers. Photograph by Helga Teiwes. Courtesy of the Arizona State Museum.

WHITE HOUSE.
WASHINGTON.

May 17th 1906

These songs cast a wholly new light on the depth and dignity of Indian thought, the simple beauty and strange charm — the charm of a vanished elder world — of Indian poetry.

Theodore Roosevelt

Letter from Theodore Roosevelt to Natalie Burlin reprinted in *The Indians' Book,* 1907.

"As I looked up through the peach trees at the low-hanging desert stars at the foot of Hopi Mesa I thought to myself—is there no one in authority who can realize before it is too late what the native life of America still holds of worth and beauty?" ("Theodore Roosevelt in Hopi-Land," 1919)

Courtesy of Harper and Brothers. Photograph by Helga Teiwes. Courtesy of the Arizona State Museum.

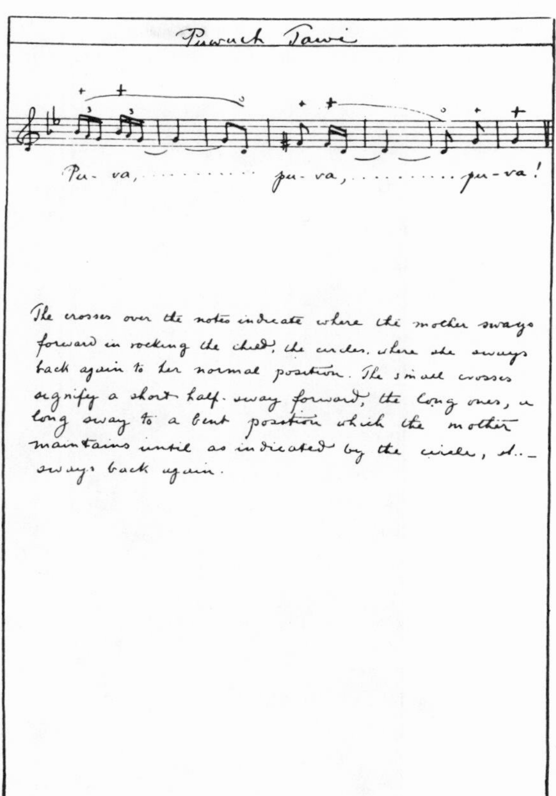

Hopi Lullaby from *The Indians' Book,* 1907.

"My good friend, when that song is sung, the baby *always* goes to sleep." (Hopi singer, quoted in "American Indian Cradle-Songs," 1921)

Courtesy of Harper and Brothers. Photographs by Helga Teiwes. Courtesy of the Arizona State Museum.

Gertrude Kurath in Otomi costume, ca. 1945.

"Any dichotomy between ethnic dance and art dance dissolves if one regards dance ethnology, not as a description or reproduction of a particular kind of dance, but as an approach toward, and a method of, eliciting the place of dance in human life." ("Panorama of Dance Ethnology," 1960)

Courtesy of Gertrude Kurath.

GERTRUDE PROKOSCH KURATH, 1903–

"It is always an esthetic treat to attend dances of the Pueblo Indians, to admire the precision and exquisite style, and to sense the deep significance behind the patterns." ("Tewa Plaza Dances: A Photo Essay," 1963)

The daughter of a pianist, Gertrude Kurath began dancing as a child. In addition to later professional training in music and dance, she studied languages, art history, drama, and choreography as a college and graduate student. Kurath has brought this unique background to studying and writing about ethnic dance since 1946 when she made her first field trip to Mexico and studied the dances of Aztec, Otomi, Zapotec, Tarascans, and Yaqui. Two meetings in 1947 led her into the study of American Indian dance-music. One was with anthropologist William Fenton who encouraged and collaborated on Kurath's Iroquois research for over a decade. The other was Edward Dozier, a native of Santa Clara Pueblo, who was studying anthropology and linguistics in Ann Arbor at the University of Michigan.

Kurath first experienced the music and dance of New Mexico's Rio Grande Pueblos in 1957 and made seven subsequent field trips to study Tewa and Keres dance-music. Her "main helper" in her Pueblo research was Antonio Garcia, whom she met "just by chance" during the February Deer Dance at his native pueblo, San Juan. A trained musician, "he was immediately enthusiastic about collaboration." Together they researched and authored *Music and Dance of the Tewa Pueblos* published in 1970 during Garcia's tenure as Governor of the pueblo. In this as in other studies, Kurath's dance ethnology research was informed by her experience in the creation and performance of dance, and her scholarship was combined with human warmth and affection for the people of her study.

EDUCATION: Student, University of Texas, 1917–19, University of Chicago, 1919–20; B.A., modern languages, 1922, M.A., art history, 1928, Bryn Mawr College; M.A., Yale School of Drama, 1929–30. Professional training in dance and music: Berlin, Bryn Mawr College.

FELLOWSHIPS AND AWARDS: Viking Fund, 1949–50; APS Research Grants, 1951–52, 1954–56, 1967–68; New York State Museum, 1952, 1955; Michigan Academy of Sciences, 1953–56; Wenner-Gren Foundation Grants, 1957–65; Award, Congress on Research in Dance, 1983.

RESEARCH: Studied dance and ethnomusicology—Mexico, Iroquois, Cherokee, Fox, New Mexico Pueblos, Anglo-American, Afro-American, 1946–86.

PROFESSIONAL ACTIVITIES: Dance instructor, choreographer, and professional dancer, 1922–46; Pageant Director, Rhode Island School of Design, 1932–41, Creative Dance Guild of Rhode Island, 1936–45, Community Music School, Rhode Island, 1935–40, Brown University, 1936–45; Research Associate, New York State Museum, 1952; Coordinator, Dance Research Center, 1957–69; Consultant, dance definitions, Webster's International Dictionary, 1958–59; Dance Critic, *Ann Arbor News*, 1961–72; Field Employee, National Museum of Canada, 1962–65, 1968–69; Consultant to several encyclopedias; Vice-President, Society for Ethnomusicology; President, Michigan Folklore Society, 1954–56.

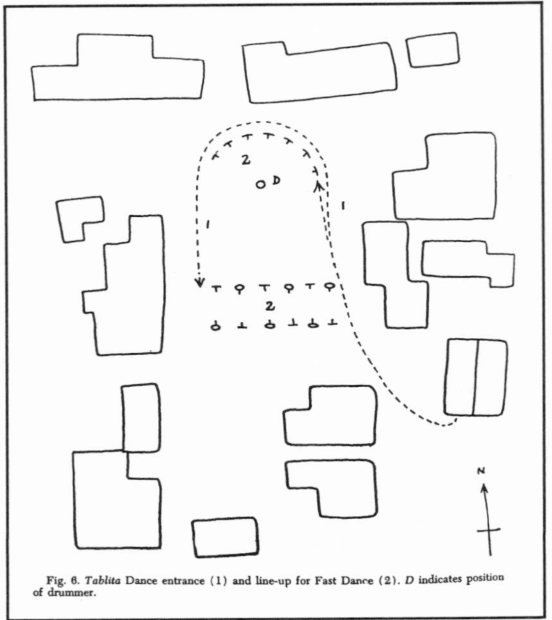

Fig. 6. *Tablita* Dance entrance (1) and line-up for Fast Dance (2). *D* indicates position of drummer.

Fig. 7. *Tablita* Dance Slow Entrance song, with texts. Some cadenzas are omitted.

Tablita Dance Plan and Entrance Song, Cochiti. (Appendix 43 in Charles H. Lange. *Cochiti: A New Mexico Pueblo, Past and Present,* 1959)

"The drums give the beat for the step and for the motion of the men who shake gourd rattles and the women who dip evergreen boughs. During a musical pause after the entrance, the singers form an arc and the dancers face each other in two lines, in preparation for the fast dance or *ayastyekuts* proper." ("Calling the Rain Gods," 1960)

Courtesy of University of Texas Press. Photograph by Helga Teiwes. Courtesy of the Arizona State Museum.

San Juan Deer Dance, 1946.

"Due to a lucky combination of circumstances, Bertha [Dutton] started my collaboration with Antonio Garcia. Early in February we settled in a charming house on Garcia Street [in Santa Fe] and had a phone installed—just in time to have Bertha phone me at [the] crack of dawn that the San Juan Deer Dance was to take place that day—Sunday." (Letter to Nancy Parezo, November 7, 1986).

Photographs by Gertrude Kurath. Courtesy of Gertrude Kurath.

Frances Gillmor, ca. 1973.

". . . in the strange dramatic serenity of the firelit ceremonies of song, I could easily forget that I myself was not a Navajo." (*Windsinger,* 1930)

Courtesy of Special Collections, University of Arizona.

FRANCES GILLMOR, 1903–

"I can't remember a time when I wasn't interested in folklore." (Interview, August 21, 1985)

Frances Gillmor was "destined" to become "a Southwesterner." When she came to Arizona in 1926 to "get away from Chicago winters," she was a newspaper reporter and established novelist. "I was writing from my childhood on, so there was never any decision about whether I should write—I just did." (Interview, August 21,1985) Her first novel, *Thumbcap Weir* (1929), dealt with her family's sardine fishery in New Brunswick.

Gillmor studied at the University of Arizona, began teaching in its English Department in 1931, and became fascinated with the native peoples of the Southwest and Mexico. Combining her training in anthropology and literature with her journalistic expertise, she produced an "expository biography," *Traders to the Navajo* (1934) with trader Louisa Wade Wetherill, who had had "such an interesting life" and "who knew how to tell a good story." While living with the Wetherills for two summers, Gillmor "went to Navajo ceremonies and took notes on everything." The result was her famous novel, *Windsinger* (1930), a book "clothed in the Navajo colors of the four directions." (Interview, August 21, 1985)

Gillmor taught at the University of Arizona for over 40 years and in 1943 founded and directed its Folklore Archive which has evolved into the Southwest Folklore Center. Her own subsequent research in Mexican folklore and folk drama produced a DD.L. in folklore and two more anthropological novels.

EDUCATION: Student, University of Chicago, 1921–23; B.A., 1928, M.A., 1931, English, University of Arizona; National School of Anthropology and History, Mexico, 1952; DD.L., folklore, Universidad Nacional Autonoma de Mexico, 1957.

FELLOWSHIPS AND AWARDS: Fellow, Folklore Institute of America, Indiana University, 1946; Guggenheim Foundation for research on Spanish folk plays, 1959–60.

RESEARCH: Arizona history; Anglo-Indian (especially Navajo) relations; Aztec history; folklore and folk drama of Jalisco, Sonora and Oaxaca.

PROFESSIONAL ACTIVITIES: Newspaper reporter, Florida, 1923–25; Teaching Fellow, English, 1928–29, Instructor to Professor Emerita, 1931–86, University of Arizona; Chairman, Folklore Committee and Director, Folklore Archives, University of Arizona, 1943–73; Visiting Professor, summer sessions, University of New Mexico, 1932–34; Associate Editor, *Arizona Quarterly*, 1945 to present; Vice-President, AFS, 1958, 1964.

Wetherill Trading Post, Kayenta, Arizona, 1926. John Wetherill at far right.

"I wrote to Louisa Wetherill and she wrote back a one line note, 'Come along,' and I went along. That was the beginning." (Interview, August 21, 1985)

Photograph by Elizabeth Hegemann. Courtesy of the University of New Mexico Press.

Virginia Roediger leaving for fieldwork in New Mexico, 1936.

"There are not many more years during which it will be possible to make such a study." (*Ceremonial Costumes of the Pueblo Indians,* 1941)

Courtesy of Virginia Roediger Johnson.

Virginia More Roediger, 1906–

"Climbing to the housetop, I looked down upon the dancing gods below. Forty-five dancers, facing each other, stretched in two lines along one side and part of each end of the plaza." (*Ceremonial Costumes of the Pueblo Indians,* 1941)

Colorado native Virginia Roediger saw her first Pueblo and Navajo dances near Coolidge, New Mexico in 1925 on an automobile trip from Denver to Los Angeles. After studying architecture at the University of Southern California, she received her M.F.A. in Theatre Design and Directing at Yale University and taught scene and costume design at the Chicago Art Institute. In 1935 Roediger decided to do her doctoral dissertation on Pueblo ceremonial costumes, took anthropology courses with Leslie Spier, and did research at the Heye Foundation. A Rockefeller Grant enabled her to do field research both in Southwest museums and at "any and all ceremonies in the various Pueblos sketching dancers and costumes." (Letter to Nancy Parezo, February 3, 1986)

Roediger's "generous and detailed investigation" was published in 1941, with her own illustrations, as *Ceremonial Costumes of the Pueblo Indians*. This comprehensive account of the evolution, fabrication, significance, and ceremonial uses of Pueblo dramatic-religious dress is unique in combining anthropological and theatrical expertise and has become an indispensable sourcebook for students of Pueblo culture. From 1942 to 1948, Roediger was a Research Associate in Anthropology at UCLA and did the illustrations for two books by Ralph Beals as well as for many leaflets published by the Santa Barbara Museum of Natural History.

EDUCATION: B.A., University of Southern California, 1928; studied architecture, University of Southern California School of Architecture; M.F.A. in theatre design and directing, Yale University, 1931; Ph.D., theatre research, Yale University, 1937.

FELLOWSHIPS: Rockefeller Grant, Pueblo research, 1936.

RESEARCH: Studied ceremonial dances among Navajo and at Hopi, Zuni, Rio Grande Pueblos, 1925–35.

PROFESSIONAL ACTIVITIES: Worked in Goodman Theatre, Chicago Art Institute, 1931–34.

Hopi Deer Dancer. (Plate 28. *Ceremonial Costumes of the Pueblo Indians,* 1941)

As Roediger observes, the simplest and most realistic form of animal impersonation is the head and pelt of a deer draped over the dancer's head and shoulders. Among the different Pueblos there are varying degrees of stylization; this observed at Hopi with a full helmet mask and dance kilt is the most complete stylization.

Courtesy of Virginia Roediger. Photograph by Helga Teiwes. Courtesy of the Arizona State Museum.

Simple costume for women. Tablita Dancer, Santo Domingo. (Plate 19. *Ceremonial Costumes of the Pueblo Indians,* 1941)

This dancer wears the Pueblo woman's traditional native homespun woolen dress or *manta.* She carries sprigs of spruce, "used on the ceremonial costume in the summer dances, evergreen is the symbol of life." Her headdress is a terraced wooden plaque or *tablita,* hence the name sometimes used for Summer Corn or Rain Dances among the Rio Grande Pueblos.

Courtesy of Virginia Roediger. Photograph by Helga Teiwes. Courtesy of the Arizona State Museum.

Applied Anthropology

There has always been a scarcity of academic jobs for cultural anthropologists, particularly for women. Increasingly over the past century, women turned to doing what is now called "applied anthropology." By working in such fields as medicine, education, mental health, and government service, many women have applied their anthropological knowledge and training to the improvement of everyday life on the reservations of the Southwest.

In the 1940s, Laura Thompson directed the Indian Education and Research Project, a unique multidisciplinary effort to assess how "good" the Indian New Deal actually was for American Indians and to understand culture and personality in depth. As Thompson has pointed out, this unusually successful project was distinguished both by the training and use of "native assistants" and by the fact that because of World War II, it was "'manned' to a conspicuous degree by women," such as Dorothea Leighton, Florence Hawley, Jane Chesky, Rosamond Spicer, Ruth Underhill, and Alice Joseph.

Laura Thompson conducting fieldwork in Guam, 1938.

"Once you get in the groove, you're an anthropologist all of the time, twenty-four hours a day, and you have a very experienced perception." (Interview, November 18, 1985)

Courtesy of Laura Thompson.

Laura Thompson, 1905–

"Nothing I had ever read about the desert prepared me for the actual experience. The Southwest shows you survival in the raw." ("Exploring American Indian Communities in Depth," 1970)

Laura Thompson studied with Alfred Kroeber and Robert Lowie at the University of California, Berkeley, where she received her Ph.D. in 1933. While studying human development at the University of Chicago in 1941, she was asked to serve as coordinator of the Indian Education and Research project. From 1941 to 1947, Thompson administered this cross-disciplinary study designed "to investigate the problems of personality development in relation to cultural patterning in the situational context of several Indian tribes . . . and to apply the results to the problem of Indian administration and education." (Interview, November 18, 1985)

Thompson came to the Southwest for the first time in 1942 to coordinate research with the Papago, Navajo, Hopi, and Zuni. "There were those who said nothing could come of a research project run by women," but Thompson and 150 scholars and Indian fieldworkers produced impressive results. The first tribal monograph was *The Hopi Way* (1944) co-authored by Thompson and Alice Joseph, whom Hopis later described as "the only ones who told the truth about the Hopi." ("Exploring American Indian Communities in Depth," 1970)

EDUCATION: B.A., anthropology, Mills College, 1927; postgraduate work at Radcliffe College, 1928, University of Chicago, 1941; Ph.D., anthropology, University of California-Berkeley, 1933.

FELLOWSHIPS AND AWARDS: Bernice P. Bishop Fellowship, Yale University, 1933–34; Institute of Pacific Relations Grant, 1934; Rosenwald Fellowship, University of Hawaii, 1938; SSRC Grant, 1939; Viking Fund Grant and Wenner-Gren Fellowship, 1948, 1951; Rockefeller Foundation Grants, 1951, 1952; LL.D., Mills College, 1973.

RESEARCH: Ethnographic and applied studies: Fiji Islands, 1933–1934; Guam, 1933–39; Hawaii, 1940–41; Hopi, 1942, 1943, 1945; Papago, 1942–46; Iceland 1952, 1960.

PROFESSIONAL ACTIVITIES: Assistant Ethnologist, Bishop Museum, 1929–34; Social Scientist, U.S. Navy, Guam, 1938–40; Social Scientist, Community Survey of Education, Hawaii, 1940–41; Coordinator of Indian Education Research Project, BIA, 1941–47; Representative of BIA to Mexico, 1942–44; Consultant, Institute of Ethnic Affairs, 1947–54; AAA Board, 1946–47; Policy Board of National Indian Institute, 1948; Professor: CUNY, 1954–56, University of North Carolina, 1957–58, North Carolina State College, 1958–60, Pennsylvania State University, 1960–61, Southern Illinois University, 1961–62, San Francisco State University, 1962–69; Consultant, various projects, including Hutterite socialization, Pennsylvania State University, 1962–85.

RESEARCH ON INDIAN EDUCATION 12/10/42

FIELD PERSONNEL (Revised)

Tribes	Reservation Supervisors	Specialists	Supervisors	Field Workers	Language
Papago	Mrs. Beulah Head, Superintendent	*Jane Chesky *Rosamund Spicer *Alice Joseph Morris Rosen (Ruth Underhill)	*Ann Clark Ruth Z. Jones	Roxana Spencer Aurelia Tossini Katherine Shorten Richard Megivern Abby Deschazo Florence Leonard Mrs. Byer (Eldon Harris) (Edna Harris)	Anita Francisco Jones Narcho
Hopi	Mr. Wayne Pratt, Education	Alice Joseph *E.A. Kennard *Wayne Pratt	Wayne Pratt S. Rosenberg Fred Kabotie	Mrs. Wayne Pratt Beryl Wagner Samuel Rosenberg Lela W. Rosenberg Mary J. Mitchell Cecile B. Wallace B.M. Lewis	Mrs. White Fred Kabotie
Navaho	Mr. George A. Boyce, Education	*Clyde Kluckhohn *Dorothea Leighton Alice Joseph *Malcolm Collier *Josephine Howard	Lisbeth Eubank	Lisbeth Eubank Rachel Jordan	Lillian Lincheze
United Pueblos	Dr. Sophie Aberle, Superintendent	*Florence Hawley Josephine Howard	Virgil Whitaker Viola Leverett Clara Gonzales	Viola Leverett Clara Gonzales Kathleen Erickson Marie Deatherage (Christine Garcia) Victor Malone (Helena Higgins) (Evelyn Page)	

UNIVERSITY OF CHICAGO - COMMITTEE ON HUMAN DEVELOPMENT
RESEARCH ON INDIAN EDUCATION

PERSONALITY CARD

Census No.____ Name____________________ (Last) (First) Community____________ School____________ No._____

Age____ Birthdate__________ Blood ______ Schooling__________ Religion________ Economic Status_______

Family	Name	Age	Village	Schooling	Religion	Occupation	Economic Status	Related Families
Father								
Mother								
Siblings								

House-mates	Name	Age	Relationship	Schooling	Religion	Occupation	Economic Status

UNIVERSITY OF CHICAGO - COMMITTEE ON HUMAN DEVELOPMENT
RESEARCH ON INDIAN EDUCATION

<u>Thematic Apperception Test</u>

<u>Purpose:</u> To get insight, through the interpretation of pictures, into certain subconscious feelings, past experiences, and social attitudes of the child.

<u>Method of administration:</u> After putting the child at ease, the tester shows the first picture to him and explains that he wants to find out if the child is able to make up a nice story about what he sees in the picture. The story should have a real beginning and an end.

While the child tells his story, he is allowed to look at the picture and to handle it, as much as he likes. The tester should note how much time elapses between the passing of the picture to the child and the first response. Likewise he should note the appearance, expressions of pleasure, fear, disgust, etc. at the sight of the picture and during its interpretation.

If the child finishes his story without giving an end to it, the tester should ask: "And what will happen later?"

There should be no time limit for the child's telling of his story. After finishing the story about the first picture, the second picture is handed to the child, and so forth.

The pictures should always be shown in the same order, according to their numbers.

If, after several pictures, the child shows symptoms of being tired, the session should be stopped and resumed on the next day or one of the following days. One single session should not last longer than 45 minutes.

The stories told by the child must be recorded <u>verbatim</u>, and the objects to which he refers should be indicated by the tester in parenthesis.

It is best to use one sheet of paper for each story and write down the number, name, sex, age and tribe of the child, and the date of the experiment at the top.

Thematic Apperception Test for Navajo children.

Indian artists such as Fred Kabotie drew pictures for the psychological testing project so that children could construct stories based on familiar subjects. The purpose of the test was "to gain insight, through the interpretation of pictures, into certain subconscious feelings, past experiences, and social attitudes of the child." (Project Directive, 1941)

Courtesy of the National Anthropological Archives, Smithsonian Institution.

(*facing page, top*) Personnel List for the Indian Education and Research Project, 1941–47.

This project involved 150 social anthropologists, sociologists, psychologists, psychiatrists, physicians, school teachers, and BIA personnel. "Perhaps the fact that the field staff consisted mostly of women played a role in the project's success. Young Indians were used to responding to women." ("Exploring American Indian Communities in Depth," 1970)

Courtesy of the National Anthropological Archives, Smithsonian Institution.

(*facing page, bottom*) Personality Cards used for profiles on children, Indian Education and Research Project.
Field workers collected information on the social background, educational record, and medical history of over one thousand children, aged 6 to 18. This information was combined with observations of actual behavior, "even to the tiniest and most insignificant-appearing details." ("Exploring American Indian Communities in Depth," 1970)

Courtesy of the National Anthropological Archives, Smithsonian Institution.

Clowns performing at a kachina dance painted by a Hopi child for a Draw-A-Man Test, 1943.

The results of the Hopi psychological tests were analyzed by Alice Joseph who spent four months on the Hopi reservation in 1943. She used her findings to "analyze the development of Hopi personality in relation to the total environment viewed in historical perspective." (*The Hopi Way,* 1944)

Courtesy of the National Anthropological Archives, Smithsonian Institution.

Hopi ceramic owl made by Elizabeth White, 1943.

"Elizabeth created it to be part of a lamp she was making, but I persuaded her to sell it to me." (Letter to Barbara Babcock and Nancy Parezo, January 5, 1986)

Courtesy of Laura Thompson. Photograph by Helga Teiwes. Courtesy of the Arizona State Museum.

Dorothea Leighton at Ramah, New Mexico, ca. 1942.

"Anthropology and psychiatry fit together because people are shaped by lifetime experiences." (Interview, November 22, 1985)

Courtesy of Dorothea Leighton.

DOROTHEA LEIGHTON, 1908–

"I think my interest in people helped a lot everywhere. I think that if people hadn't liked me back, so to speak, I wouldn't have been able to do half what I did." (Interview, November 22, 1985)

Dorothea Cross received her M.D. from Johns Hopkins in 1936. A year later she married fellow student Alexander Leighton, who decided they should go into psychiatry. During their residency, they attended the Kardiner-Linton seminars on anthropology and psychoanalysis and developed an interest in "what kind of people had what kind of problems." (Interview, November 21, 1985) With Clyde Kluckhohn's encouragement, the Leightons went to work with "his" Navajo at Ramah, New Mexico in 1939. From the Navajo as from the Eskimo, they successfully collected life histories—"if you can get a man and woman team I think you get a better balance." (Interview, November 22, 1985)

Their field experiences as doctors doing anthropology led Leighton to write *The Navajo Door* (1944), an introduction to Navajo life for doctors and BIA personnel later described as the beginning of medical anthropology. During the 1940s, Leighton worked with the Navajo and the Zuni for the Indian Education and Research Project. With Kluckhohn's collaboration, she published the results of her research in *Children of the People* (1947), an important study of Navajo culture and personality.

EDUCATION: B.A., Bryn Mawr College, 1930; M.D., Johns Hopkins University School of Medicine, 1936; certified, National Board of Medical Examiners, 1939; graduate work in anthropology, Columbia University, 1939.

FELLOWSHIPS AND AWARDS: SSRC International Fellow and Training Fellowship in Anthropology, 1939–40; Guggenheim Foundation, 1946–47.

RESEARCH: Ethnographic and applied research—Navajo, Eskimo, Zuni.

PROFESSIONAL ACTIVITIES: Chemistry technician, Johns Hopkins Hospital, 1930–32; Intern, Baltimore City Hospitals, 1936–37; Resident in psychiatry, Johns Hopkins Hospital, 1937–42; Special Physician, BIA, 1942–45; Assistant Professor, Child Development and Family Relations, Cornell University, 1949–52; Research Associate, Department of Anthropology, Cornell University, 1952–58; Associate Professor, Clinical Psychiatry, Cornell University, 1958–65; Professor of Mental Health, School of Public Health, University of North Carolina, 1965–74; Department Chair, 1972–74; Instructor, Forum for Educators in Community Psychiatry, Duke University, 1967–71; Visiting Professor, Anthropology, University of California, Berkeley, 1981–82; Vice-President, American Association of Social Psychiatry, 1971.

"Health Education in the Field." (*The Navaho Door,* 1944)

"Nobody took any trouble to talk to doctors in the Indian Health Service about the Indians they were treating." (Interview, November 21, 1985)

Photograph by Helen N. Post. Courtesy of Harvard University Press.

New Hogan-style Day School Buildings at Shonto, 1934.

Following Reichard's and Leighton's pioneering work, many anthropologists have worked with native educational systems. Lucy Adams supervised BIA schools on the Navajo reservation in the 1950s.

Photograph by Elizabeth Hegemann. Courtesy of the University of New Mexico Press.

Archaeology

Centuries of continuous habitation and the combination of many well-preserved prehistoric ruins and historic Native American cultures have attracted numerous archaeologists to the Southwest and enabled the training of countless more in summer field schools. Although they came to archaeology later than to ethnology, women have made important additions both to regional culture histories and to archaeological theory and method, especially ceramic analysis. They have also been instrumental in preserving archaeological resources in many areas such as Mesa Verde and Chaco Canyon. Despite their training and expertise, few women archaeologists have held academic appointments, most of them working in museums and more recently on contract archaeology projects.

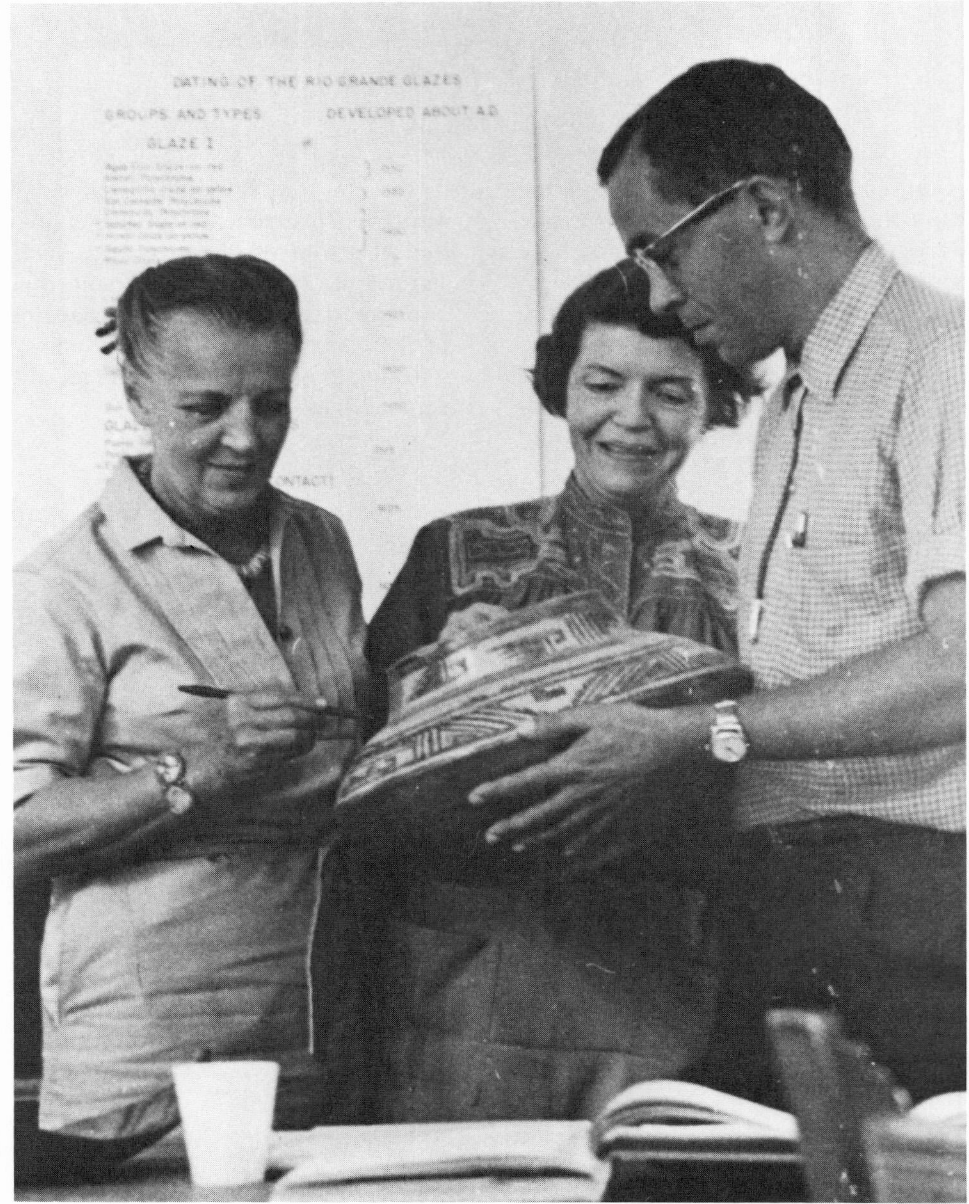

Florence Hawley Ellis, Marjorie Lambert, and Stewart Peckham at the Eighth Annual Southwestern Ceramic Conference, Museum of New Mexico, September 16, 1966.

"I wanted to live out here and be with my Indian friends and the archaeology that went with them." (Interview, August 4, 1985)

Courtesy of the Museum of Northern Arizona.

Florence Hawley Ellis, 1906–

"Dedication to anthropology is like dedication to one's religion; it is a way of life." (Interview, August 4, 1985)

Florence Hawley Ellis was one of the first women to receive a Ph.D. in archaeology and to use both statistics and tree-ring dating in her analyses. A pioneer in ethnoarchaeology, she is known both for her work at the Anasazi ruin of Chetro Ketl in Chaco Canyon and her studies of Keresan kinship and social organization. "My relationship to the Pueblo people has been influenced by the fact that I'm a woman. . . . If you remain a woman in their eyes, they'll accept you. Women have a definite place and expected behavior in Pueblo society. Their place is more equal than in our society." (Interview, August 4, 1985)

Since the mid-1950s, Ellis has used her considerable energies and expertise to help establish Pueblo claims to land and water rights. Believing that "you ought to be willing to give back to the Indians whatever they can use of your understanding of things," she has helped Zia, Santa Ana, Jemez, Nambe, Taos, Acoma, Laguna, Hopi, and Santo Domingo. "I think the Pueblo men think of women as being good advisors." (Interview, August 4, 1985)

Never interested in administration, Ellis devoted her time to research and teaching. Through the University of New Mexico field schools and classes, Ellis introduced numerous students to Southwestern archaeology and taught them "anthropology that wasn't just out of books." (Interview, August 5, 1985)

EDUCATION: B.A., 1927, M.A., 1928, archaeology, University of Arizona; Ph.D., anthropology, University of Chicago, 1934.
FELLOWSHIPS AND AWARDS: Scholarship to attend University of Chicago, 1932; Doctor of Philosophy, University of New Mexico, 1988.
RESEARCH: Work on Salado sites and pottery analysis, late 1920s; archaeological excavations and dendrochronological work in Chaco Canyon, 1929–33, 1985; dendrochronological fieldwork in Midwest and South, 1934; Director, University of New Mexico field schools, 1956, 1959, 1960, 1962–64; archaeological excavations, surveys and oral history projects for various Pueblo land claims cases, 1970s.
PROFESSIONAL ACTIVITIES: Research Assistant, Arizona State Museum, 1928–29; Instructor, University of Arizona, 1929–33; Assistant Professor to Professor Emerita, University of New Mexico, 1934–present; Part-time Associate Professor, University of Chicago, 1937–40; AAA Elections Committee, 1948; Adjunct Professor, Eckerd College, 1973; Consultant, New Mexico Archaeological Project, University of New Mexico and NPS, 1972.

A. E. Douglass, pioneer in dendrochronology.

Ellis was A. E. Douglass's assistant in 1930–31. "I decided that this would be a good thing to be in because if you could have a specialty you were more likely to be wanted, which was a point especially for a female." (Interview, August 4, 1985)

Courtesy of Special Collections, University of Arizona.

(*facing page, top*) Florence Hawley Ellis, Gladys Phare, Emil W. Haury, and Clara Lee Tanner at the University of Arizona's field school, 1926.

The University of Arizona's first graduates in archaeology (1928), Florence Hawley Ellis, Clara Lee Tanner and Emil Haury have all had distinguished careers in anthropology. "Cummings said he was expanding the department, and that we could all have jobs. So we worked hard and got our M.A.s in one year." (Interview, August 4, 1985)

Courtesy of the Arizona Historical Society.

(*facing page, bottom, left*) Pinto Polychrome bowl, Tank Wash, Roosevelt Lake, Arizona. Arizona State Museum, Cat. No. GP 7743.

(*bottom, right*) Tonto Polychrome ceramic bowl, Salado, ca. A.D. 1300–1450, Upper Pinto Ruin, Gila County, Arizona. Arizona State Museum, Cat. No. GP 8635. Collected by Gila Pueblo Foundation, 1929. Gift of Harold S. Gladwin, 1950.

As a child, Ellis collected pottery from Salado ruins along the Middle Gila River. Using pots like this, she and her father studied southwestern pottery through chemical analyses of the pigments.

Photograph by Helga Teiwes. Courtesy of the Arizona State Museum.

Students of Byron Cummings and A. E. Douglass. (*left to right*) Emil Haury, Florence Hawley Ellis, Clara Lee Tanner, and Waldo Wedel at the 50th reunion of the first dendrochronology class at the Arizona State Museum, February, 1985. Museum Director Raymond Thompson front right.

In the early 1930s, Ellis applied the new technique of tree-ring dating to Chetro Ketl, a ruin in Chaco Canyon. She pioneered in the dating of charcoal samples from cooking fires and also extended the dating method to the Mississippi River valley.

The cycloscope was created by Douglass in the 1930s to look for cycles in a series of past events, such as the growth of the rings in a tree.

Photograph by Helga Teiwes. Courtesy of the Arizona State Museum.

Florence Hawley Ellis supervising University of New Mexico's field school at Chaco Canyon, 1964.

Since 1934 when Ellis joined the faculty at the University of New Mexico, she has taught numerous students the finer points of archaeological field techniques. Bertha Dutton and Robert Lister were in her first class.

Courtesy of the Museum of New Mexico.

Marjorie Lambert, 1932.

"I don't see how you could regret a career in anthropology. . . . Even if you don't make anthropology your major field of endeavor, the background in anthropology is perfect for so many other professions." (Interview, September 2, 1985)

Courtesy of Marjorie Lambert.

MARJORIE F. LAMBERT, 1910–

"I just like the challenge that prehistory seemed to give, the mystery of it, and finding out about people—why they think the way they do, and what makes history." (Interview, September 2, 1985)

Colorado native Marjorie Lambert was introduced to archaeology by Edgar Lee Hewett and received her M.A. in 1931 from the University of New Mexico, where she was an Instructor in Archaeology and Museology until 1937. As curator at the Museum of New Mexico for over thirty years, her primary interests centered upon the prehistory, history, and ethnology of the Southwest—"my archaeology would be nothing without the present-day Indians." (Interview, September 2, 1985)

Lambert has most enjoyed fieldwork, but believes that archaeologists "have a responsiblity to report on what [they] uncover." In addition to publishing many papers, she has given countless lectures and organized many exhibits introducing New Mexico's Indian and Hispanic peoples to the general public. Through the Archaeological Society of New Mexico, Lambert worked for many years to foster a productive relationship between amateur and professional archaeologists, believing that "archaeologists have a message because those who don't appreciate the past are right in line to repeat it." (Interview, September 2, 1985)

EDUCATION: B.A., Colorado College, 1930; M.A., anthropology, University of New Mexico, 1931.
FELLOWSHIPS AND AWARDS: Alice Zan Diest Award for exellence in Social Studies, Colorado College, 1930; Pi Gamma Mu, honorary social science fraternity; Graduate Fellowship, University of New Mexico, 1930–34; School of American Research grant, 1934–37, grant-in-aid, 1960; Honorary Life Member, Archaeological Society of New Mexico; Honorary Life Member, School of American Research; Curator Emeritus Award, Museum of New Mexico, 1984; SAA 50th Award for Outstanding Contributions to American Archaeology, 1985.
RESEARCH: Archaeology, both prehistoric and historic, especially sites of Kuaua, Paa-ko, Otowi, Puaray, Yuque-Yunque, and Luna and Hildago counties in New Mexico,and Sonora, Mexico; ethnography in northern and central Rio Grande, New Mexico, 1930–70s.
PROFESSIONAL ACTIVITIES: Teaching Assistant, University of New Mexico, 1931; Instructor, New Mexico Highlands University, 1932–36; Research Associate, School of American Research, 1932; Field Supervisor, University of New Mexico field school, 1934–37; Preparator, 1937–38, Curator of Archaeology, 1938–59, in charge of Palace of Governors, 1955–64, Curator of Anthropology and Exhibits, 1959–63, Curator of Research Division, 1963–69, Museum of New Mexico; Research Associate Professor, Eastern New Mexico University, 1969–72; Research Associate, School of American Research, 1969–78; Board, School of American Research, 1972–present; Chair, Picuris Pueblo Museum; Trustee, 1948–78, Secretary 1948–49, Chair 1949–50, Indian Arts Fund; Secretary, Archaeological Society of New Mexico, 1939–59; Trustee, Spanish Colonial Society, 1970–present.

Marjorie Lambert's field school at Tecolate Ruin, 1932. Lambert at top left.

Lambert supervised several University of New Mexico-Museum of New Mexico field schools in the 1930s. She preferred being in the field to any other activity. "Once I got my feet and hands in the dirt I never left." (Interview, September 2, 1985)

Courtesy of Marjorie Lambert.

Well excavation and reconstruction in the patio of the Palace of the Governors, Santa Fe, New Mexico, 1956. (*left to right*) Marjorie Lambert, Ray Ghent, Bernie Valdez.

Lambert's concern for the preservation of Santa Fe's unique historical and architectural character led her into historic as well as prehistoric archaeology. She both supervised and wrote about the excavations at the Palace of the Governors.

Photograph by Arthur Taylor. Courtesy of the Museum of New Mexico.

Bertha Dutton at the Las Madres site in Galisteo Basin, New Mexico, ca. 1963.

"The Indians have molded me and I want them to know it." (Interview, August 2, 1985)

Photograph by Paul Theit. Courtesy of Bertha Dutton and the Museum of New Mexico.

BERTHA P. DUTTON, 1903–

"I spent half a century setting trails around the Southwest." (Interview, August 2, 1985)

Bertha P. Dutton has spent a lifetime preserving both the archaeological and ethnological heritage of New Mexico. She came to the Southwest in 1932, after several years as a secretary in Nebraska. Using the settlement from a traffic accident, she purchased a Model A Ford and registered for the University of New Mexico's field school under the direction of Edgar L. Hewett.

In 1936, Dutton joined the Museum of New Mexico staff as Hewett's assistant and three years later persuaded him to create the position of Curator of Ethnology—"you had to invent your job in so many places." (Interview August 2, 1985) After retiring in 1966, she became director of the Museum of Navaho Ceremonial Art and revived this institution that had declined following Mary Cabot Wheelwright's death.

In both her museum work and her publications, Dutton has dedicated herself to popularizing anthropology. From 1946 to 1957, she organized a series of Archaeological Mobile Camps for Senior Girl Scouts and "helped educate hundreds of children," one of whom is ethnobotanist Vorsila Bohrer. (Interview, August 2, 1985)

EDUCATION: Studied part-time, University of Nebraska, 1925–30; B.A., 1935, M.A., 1937, anthropology, University of New Mexico; Ph.D., anthropology, Columbia University, 1952.

FELLOWSHIPS AND AWARDS: Alice Fletcher Traveling Fellow, 1935; School of American Research Fellowships, 1935, 1950; Blodgett Research Fellowship, 1953–54; American Association of University Women Grant, 1953; NSF Grant-in-Aid, 1962–63; Wenner-Gren Foundation Grant, 1962–63; Columbus Explorer Fund Grant, 1964, 1965, 1968; Certificate of Appreciation, Indian Arts and Crafts Board, 1967; LL.D., New Mexico State University, 1973.

RESEARCH: Archaeology in Southwest since 1933, especially in New Mexico; Peru and Bolivia, 1935; Mexico and Guatemala, 1953–54, 1962–63; Europe, 1964; South America, 1965; Japan, 1968.

PROFESSIONAL ACTIVITIES: Secretary, Child Welfare Department, Nebraska, 1928–32; Secretary, Anthropology Department, University of New Mexico, 1933–36; Administrative Assistant, 1936–39, Curator of Ethnology, 1939–59, Instructor of TV and adult classes, 1947–57, Curator of Exhibits, 1960–62, Head, Division of Research, 1962–65, Museum of New Mexico; AAA Executive Council, 1947; AAA Elections Committee, 1948; Instructor, St. Michael's College, 1965; Director, Museum of Navajo Ceremonial Art, 1966–75; Board Member, Southwest Association on Indian Affairs, 1959–1976, Fred Harvey Fine Art Foundation, 1971–1976; NPS Advisory Board, 1973–78.

Hulda Hobbs, Jean Cady, Marjorie Lambert, and Bertha Dutton at the Alibates site in west Texas, ca. 1935.

Marjorie Lambert was Bertha Dutton's first instructor in archaeology at the 1932 University of New Mexico field school in Chaco Canyon. Since then, these two women have collaborated on many archaeological projects.

Courtesy of Bertha Dutton.

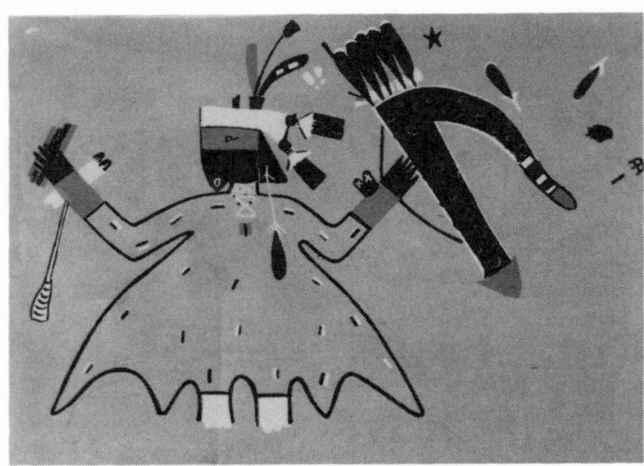

Kuaua Mural

In 1935 Hewett assigned Dutton the task of discovering the identification, origin, and meaning of the various figures in the famous painted murals at Kuaua. With the assistance of Pueblo Indians, she was able to reconstruct the Anasazi pantheon.

Courtesy of Bertha Dutton.

Model of Dutton's Model A Truck, "Bert's Bouncing Buggy" by Ed Dittert.

Berty or Bert "as everyone calls [her]," was famous for her excursions in her 1928 Model A Ford. "When Dr. Hewett brought me here [Santa Fe] to work at the museum, he said I would get $100 a month. He told me to save a little every month. I did—$10 per month." With this she purchased her "buggy" which she had "until about three years ago." (Interview, August 2, 1985)

Model courtesy of Bertha Dutton. Photograph by Helga Teiwes. Courtesy of the Arizona State Museum.

Site plan of Las Madres, Galisteo Basin, New Mexico.

Dutton received a Wenner-Gren Foundation grant in 1963–1964 to excavate Las Madres (LA25) in the Galisteo Basin. She was interested in prehistoric migration patterns in northern New Mexico.

Drawing by Alice Wesche. Courtesy of Bertha Dutton and the Museum of New Mexico.

Anna Shepard, curator of anthropology at the San Diego Museum of Man, posing with the Mimbres pottery she collected in New Mexico, 1928.

"You are always reaching out for interpretations of what you observe and for correlations with other aspects of the broader problem." (Letter from A.V. Kidder to Shepard, July 26, 1933)

Anna O. Shepard Archives. Courtesy of the University of Colorado Museum.

Anna O. Shepard, 1903–1973

"A puzzle challenges us, it entertains and excites, and it holds our interest as long as we have resource to devise fresh methods of attack." ("Cell Tempered Pottery" 1936)

Anna Shepard came to the Southwest in 1923 as a student at the School of American Research's Gran Quivira field school. Interested in discovering how pottery could help solve anthropological puzzles, she began with a study of Zuni vocabulary for pottery and pottery design. Later as a student at the Chaco Canyon field school, "she found out that nobody knew anything about the technology of pottery, so she specialized in that field." (Bertha Dutton, Interview, August 2, 1985)

A dedicated geochemist and mineralogist noted for her comprehension of analytical processes, rigorous methodology, and her quest for scientific accuracy, Shepard contributed significantly to our knowledge of the technology of southwestern and mesoamerican pottery. Her book, *Ceramics for the Archaeologist* (1956), is the definitive guide to ceramic analysis and reflects her broad anthropological perspective.

Shepard was one of the first anthropologists to undertake what later became known as ethnoarchaeology. She studied pottery making in the Rio Grande Pueblos, concentrating on firing techniques at San Ildefonso and Santa Clara. She used this information to analyze the pottery unearthed at Pecos by Alfred V. Kidder.

EDUCATION: B.A., anthropology, University of Nebraska, 1926; postgraduate studies: in optical crystallography at Claremont College, 1930; in chemical spectroscopy at New York University, 1937; M.I.T., 1940; Ph.D., chemistry, University of Colorado, 1942.

FELLOWSHIPS AND AWARDS: Fellow, School of American Research, 1924; Meritorious Service Award and Honor Award for Superior Service, USGS, 1970, 1971.

RESEARCH: School of American Research Field School at Gran Quivera and Jemez, 1923; Mimbres region, 1927–1929; University of New Mexico Field School at Chaco Canyon, 1929; archaeological and ethnological ceramic research in northern Rio Grande region, 1930–37; laboratory research in archaeological ceramic technology, 1937–68; Awatobi expedition, Harvard University, 1940; Mesa Verde, 1947–1948; research in Israel, British Honduras, Mexico, Guatemala, and India.

PROFESSIONAL ACTIVITIES: Curator of Ethnography, San Diego Museum of Man, 1926–30; Research Associate in ceramics, Laboratory of Anthropology, 1930–37; Ceramicist, Carnegie Institute of Washington, 1936–68; Geologist, USGS, 1957–70; Visiting Scholar, Hebrew University, 1966; Instructor, seminar in ceramic technology, University of Missouri, 1969; numerous lectures at University of Colorado; participant in Wenner-Gren Conference, "Ceramics and Man," 1961.

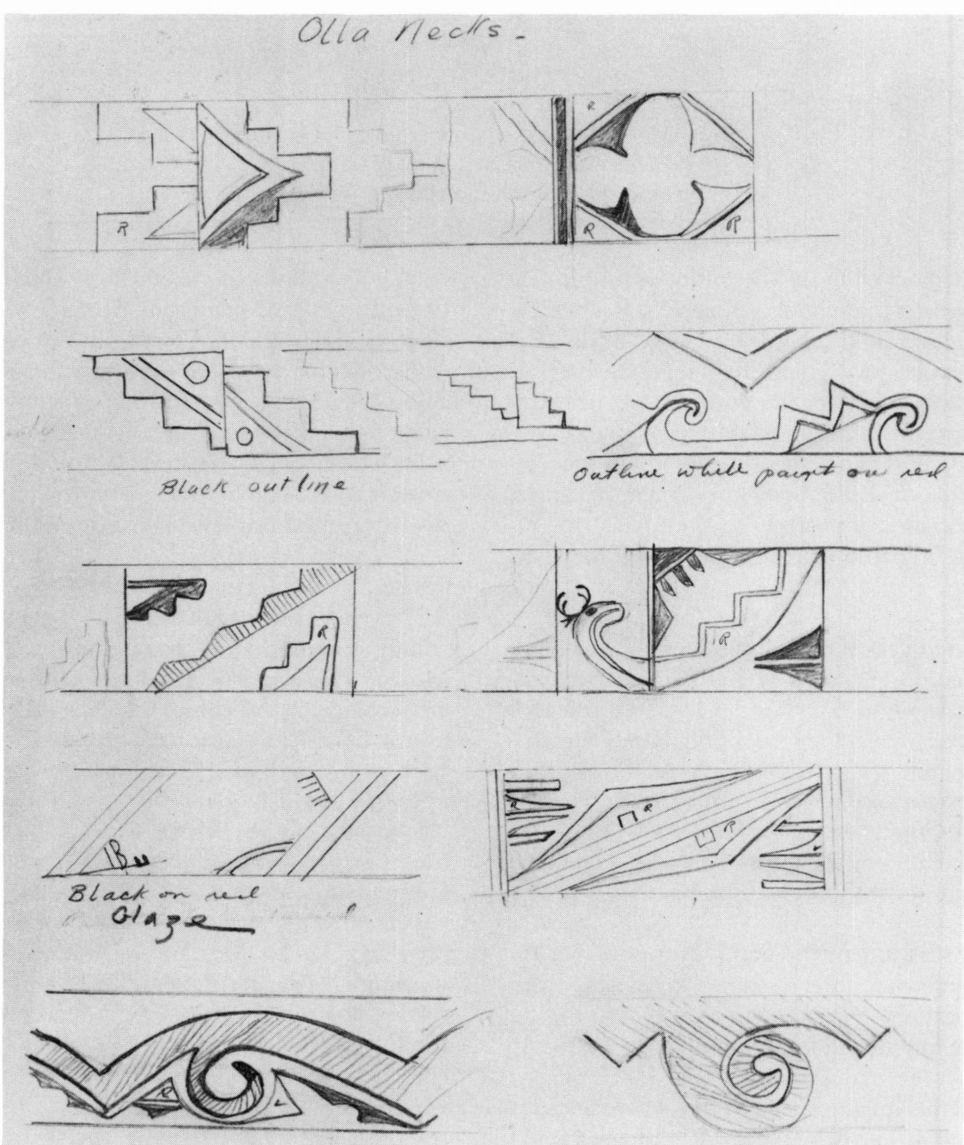

Sketches of olla necks by Anna Shepard, ca. 1930.

Anna Shepard's detailed chemical analyses laid the foundation for petrographic analysis. She also kept detailed records of the artistic qualities of every pot and potsherd she analyzed.

Anna O. Shepard Archives. Courtesy of the University of Colorado Museum.

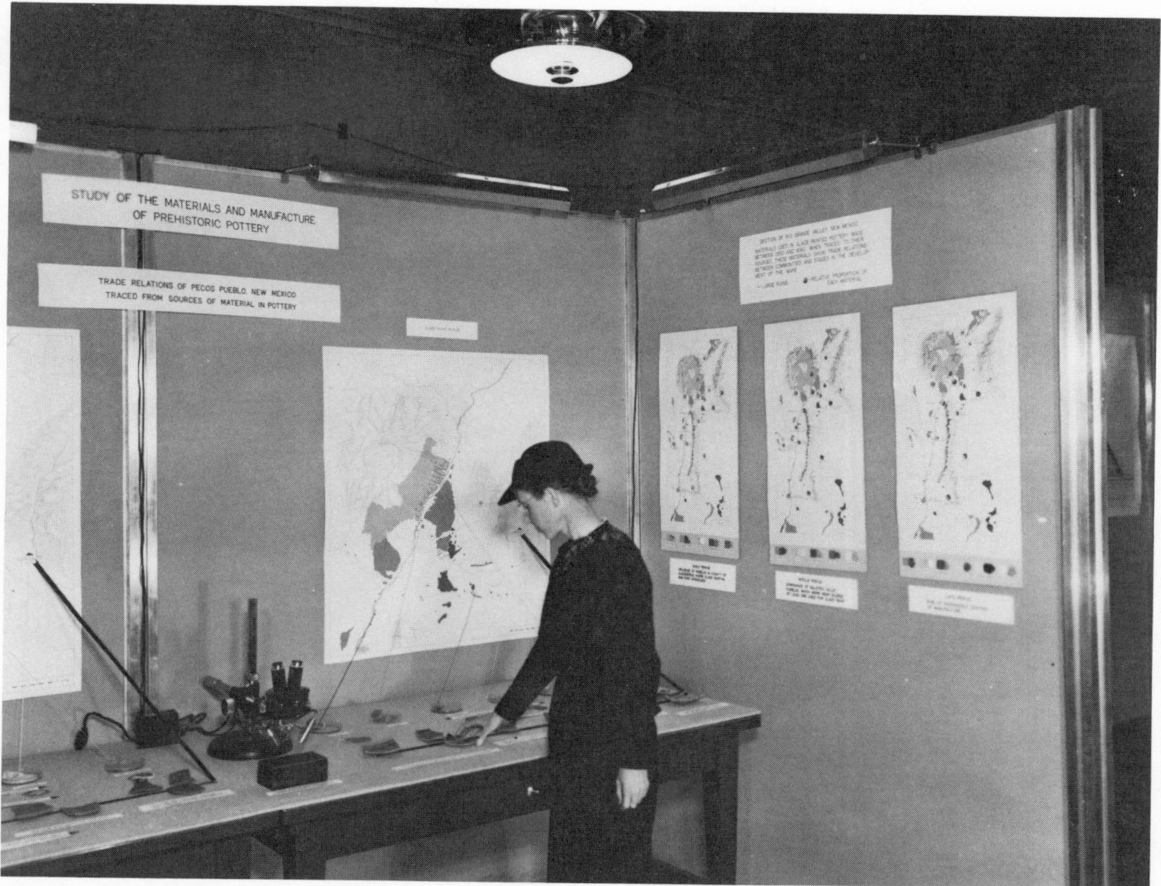

Anna Shepard examining Pecos exhibits at Museum of New Mexico.

From 1931 to 1936, Shepard worked as a research associate at the Laboratory of Anthropology specializing in petrographic analysis of Pecos ceramics. "Part of the fascination of ceramics lies in the variety of material and the complexity of processes that are employed." ("Archaeological Ceramic Technology," n.d.)

Courtesy of the Carnegie Institute, Washington D.C.

Dorothy Keur and three colleagues at Big Bead Mesa, 1940.

"My fieldwork was a picnic with a purpose." (Interview, August 6, 1985)

Courtesy of Dorothy Keur.

Dorothy Keur, 1904–

"Here were these great marvelous ruins, and here were Navajos living their own kind of life."
(Interview, August 6, 1985)

Dorothy Keur "stumbled into anthropology" and considered herself fortunate to attend Boas's last class at Columbia University. While teaching full-time at Hunter College and working on her Ph.D. at Columbia, she attended Edgar Lee Hewett's field school at Chaco Canyon and developed an interest in southwestern archaeology. Keur combined her interests in ethnology and archaeology in a study of Navajo origins and acculturation. Her excavations at Big Bead Mesa and in the Gobernador area helped document Navajo life and Navajo-Pueblo relations in the Pueblo refugee period (1700–1800).

Dorothy Keur has spent thirty-seven years teaching and expanding the anthropology department at Hunter College. "I really feel that my chief contribution has been in teaching thousands upon thousands of students. . . . For me, this was more rewarding than just having additional publications or becoming famous in one line or another." (Interview, August 6, 1985)

EDUCATION: B.A., anthropology, Hunter College, 1925; M.A., 1928, Ph.D., 1941, anthropology, Columbia University.
FELLOWSHIPS AND AWARDS: Grants from the Smithsonian Institution (through Dr. Matthew Stirling) and from Columbia University-Southwest Society (through Dr. Elsie Clews Parsons) for Navajo archaeology, 1939, 1940; Fulbright Fellowship for community studies research in the Netherlands, 1953; Wenner-Gren Foundation Grant for community studies research in Windward Islands, Dutch West Indies, 1955–56; New Mexico Governor's Award of Honor for Historic Preservation, 1986.
RESEARCH: Archaeology, Chaco Canyon, with University of New Mexico field school, 1931; archaeology on Navajo origins on Big Bead Mesa and in Gobernador area, 1939–40; ethnology and community studies in Netherlands, 1951–53 and Dutch West Indies, 1955–56.
PROFESSIONAL ACTIVITIES: Laboratory Assistant, Hunter College, 1925–28; Instructor to Professor Emerita, Hunter College, 1928–86; AES Board, 1946–47; Chairperson, Department of Sociology and Anthropology, Hunter College, 1947–50; Executive Board Member, AAA, 1945–48; Consultant, Committee on Disaster Research, NRC, 1952; Chair, Anthropology section, New York Academy of Sciences, Fellow, 1948; President, 1954–55, AES.

Hunter College of the City of New York
695 Park Avenue

October 31, 1940.

My dear Dr. Parsons,

Enclosed, kindly find an itemized expense account of last summer's field trip, and a copy of the brief report sent to the Smithsonian Institution, as required by the terms of our permit to excavate on government lands.

In a few weeks, when I have arranged a good synoptic exhibit of material, I hope you will come to examine it, and to stimulate me with questions difficult to answer!

With warm personal regards,
Sincerely, Dorothy L. Keur

EXPENSE ACCOUNT.

Acct. No. 030-1000

Funds,- Anthropological Research, 1940-41,
and Elsie Clews Parsons Gift.

Date 1940		Receipt No.	Item	Where Purchased.		Amt.
June	8-	1	1 Camp Stove	New York		$ 8.14
"	8	2	Postage on Food Specimens	Lab. of Anthro. Sante Fe, N. Mex.		1.30
"	20	3	1 Tube	Ogallala, Neb.		1.65
"	20	4	Clean. Carborotur &c	Brush, Colo.		.75
"	20	5	Tube, Oil, Tire	Colo.		6.28
"	22	6	Food Supplies	Albuquerque, N. Mex		3.51
"	24	7	Dirt Cap	Sante Fe, N. Mex.		.56
"	25	8	File	"	"	.33
"	25	9	Dirt Motor	"	"	.15
"	25	10	Cap	"	"	.18
"	25	11	Repair Short	"	"	.61
"	26	12	Oil and Gas	Gallup, N. Mex.		4.04
July	1	13	100 lbs. Sugar (for tent)	Lybrooks, N. Mex.		5.00
"	2	14	Navaho Assistant	Gobernados,	"	11.00
June	26	15	Install. Distrib. Points	Gallup	"	1.18
"	28	16	Auto Supplies	Albuquerque	"	1.21
"	28	17	Wrench	"	"	.46
"	28	18	Food Supplies	Farmington,	"	23.32
"	29	19	2 Tires, Camp Stool and Pillow	Albuquerque	"	15.37
"	22	20	Car Supplies, Jack, Chains &c	"	"	10.27
July	1	21	1 pair Levis	"	"	.70
				Forward, $		96.01

Letter to Elsie Clews Parsons and List of Expenses for 1940.

Dorothy Keur's Big Bead Mesa project was funded by Elsie Clews Parsons. "I still can see her coming to the seminars at Columbia, being driven by her chauffeur, getting out with a long fur coat and Indian beaded moccasins on her feet. She was a great character." (Interview, August 6, 1985)

Courtesy of the American Philosophical Society.

(*facing page, top*) Floor plan and cross sections, Big Bead Mesa. (Figures 1–3, *Big Bead Mesa*, 1941)

Keur's advisor at Columbia University was archaeologist Duncan Strong. "I wrote a paper for his course on Navajo origins. He thought it would be a good paper if it had some archaeological evidence in it. None had really been done, so he said I should go do it. So, that is how I went into doing the Big Bead Mesa study." (Interview, August 6, 1985)

Courtesy of the Society for American Archaeology. Photograph by Helga Teiwes. Courtesy of the Arizona State Museum.

(*facing page, bottom*) General view of Big Bead Mesa and environs from a hill east of camp.

"We found Big Bead Mesa, which was named thus because it was strewn with brachiopod fossils that looked like big beads. Shells are seen as potential beads by the Navajo." (Interview, August 6, 1985)

Photograph by and courtesy of Dorothy Keur.

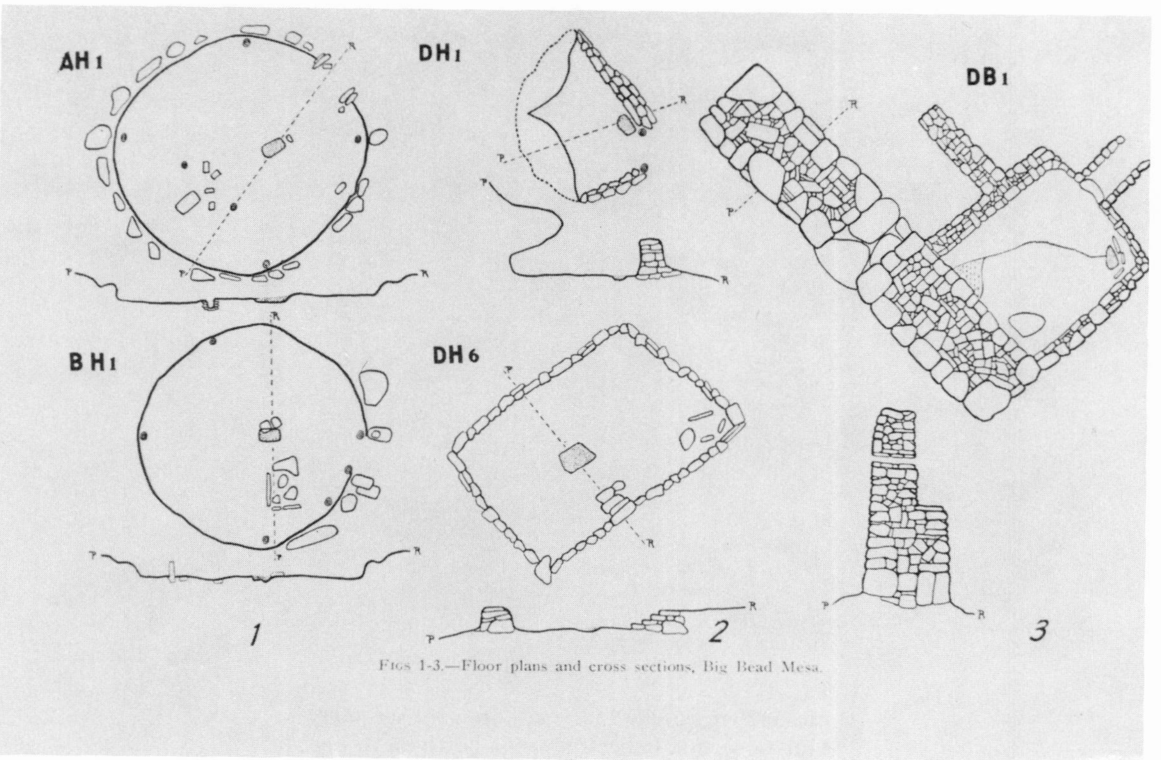

Figs 1-3.—Floor plans and cross sections, Big Bead Mesa.

Helen Heinze, Billy Marquard, Irmgard Weitlaner (Johnson), and Isabel Kelly on a beach in Mexico, ca. 1945.

Following in the footsteps of Ralph Beals, Kelly spent most of her career in northern Mexico. She lived in Mexico from the early 1940s until her death.

Courtesy of Gayle Hartmann.

Isabel Kelly, 1906–1984

"It wouldn't be any fun if the solution to every problem were obvious." (Letter to Frances Gillmor, August 5, 1947)

Isabel Kelly studied cultural anthropology with Alfred Kroeber and Carl Sauer at the University of California at Berkeley. Her fieldwork was with the groups in northern California in the late 1920s and the Southern Paiute in the early 1930s. Unlike most anthropologists whose interest in archaeology led them to ethnology, Kelly developed an interest in prehistoric cultures after her ethnographic experiences. In 1937 and 1938, she excavated the Hodges Site for The Gila Pueblo Archaeological Foundation. These excavations were essential to understanding Hohokam culture in southern Arizona. All subsequent publications dealing with Tucson Basin archaeology are based on Kelly's work.

After working in Arizona, Kelly moved south to concentrate on the archaeology of western Mexico, especially Sinaloa and Jalisco. This region was virtually unknown when Kelly began her work. Her research has extended our knowledge about contacts between the Greater Southwest and Mesoamerica.

EDUCATION: B.A., 1925, M.A., 1927, Ph.D., 1932, anthropology, University of California–Berkeley.
FELLOWSHIPS AND AWARDS: NRC Fellow, 1931–32; Laboratory of Anthropology Scholarship in Archaeology, 1929; Laboratory of Anthropology Fellowship, 1931–32; Guggenheim Foundation Fellowship for research in Mexico, 1940–41, 1942–43; Carnegie Institute and APS Grant, 1943–44; Rockefeller Foundation Grant, 1966; Wenner-Gren Foundation Grants, 1967, 1971; National Geographic Society Research Grant, 1968–70.
RESEARCH: Archaeology at Pecos, 1929; ethnography with Southern Paiute, Coast Miwok, 1920s–30s; archaeology, Hohokam, 1937–38; archaeology, western Mexico, especially Colima and Jalisco, 1930s–50s; applied anthropology—western Mexico, 1950s.
PROFESSIONAL ACTIVITIES: Research Associate, University of California-Berkeley, 1929–30, 1933–36; Executive Council, AAA, 1931–42; AAA Representative to 7th American Scientific Congress in Mexico City, 1936; Research Associate, Gila Pueblo, Globe, Az., 1936–38; Supervisor, Archaeological Research, Institute of Social Anthropology, BAE, Smithsonian Institution, 1945–51; Anthropologist, International Cooperative Administration, AID, U.S. Operations Mission, 1952–60; Research Consultant, Arizona State Museum, 1961–76.

1937–1938 excavations at the Hodges Site (Ariz. AA:12:18), Tucson, Arizona, with House 61 in the foreground.

Photograph by Isabel Kelly. Courtesy of the Arizona State Museum.

(*facing page, top, left*) Carved stone vessel. Hohokam, Rincon Phase, ca. A.D. 900–1100. Hodges Site. Arizona State Museum Cat. No. A-7285.

(*top, right*) Tanque Verde Red-on-brown sheep effigy ceramic vessel. Hohokam, Classic Period; ca. A.D. 1200–1300. Collected by Isabel Kelly from the Hodges Site, 1936. Gift of Wetmore Hodges, Arizona State Museum Cat. No. A-9240.

Photograph by Helga Teiwes. Courtesy of the Arizona State Museum.

(*facing page, bottom, left*) Shell bracelet in the shape of a frog. Hohokam, Colonial-Sedentary Periods, ca. A.D. 500–1200. Collected by Isabel Kelly at the Hodges Site, 1937. Gift of Wetmore Hodges, Arizona State Museum Cat. No. A-7305.

(*bottom, right*) Shell pendant in the shape of a frog. Hohokam, Colonial-Sedentary Periods, ca. A.D. 900–1300. Collected by Isabel Kelly at the Hodges Site, 1937. Gift of Wetmore Hodges, Arizona State Museum Cat. No. A-7311.

Photograph by Helga Teiwes. Courtesy of the Arizona State Museum.

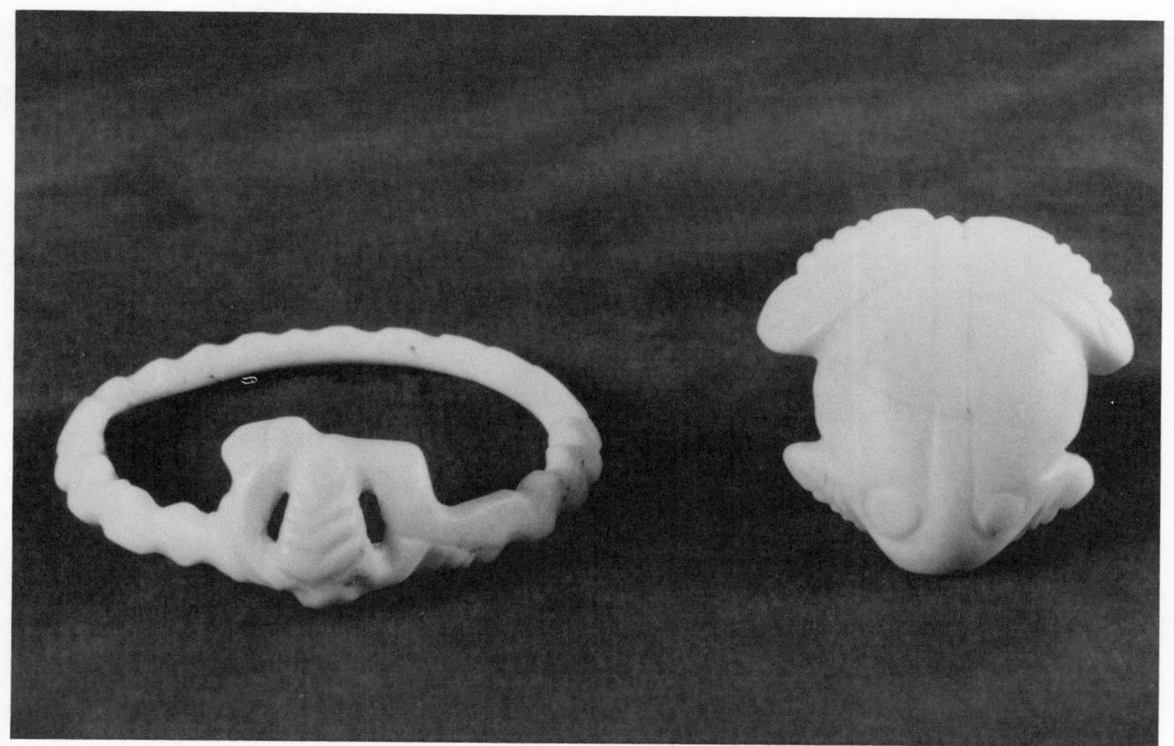

Marie Wormington on archaeological excavation, 1938.

"Once I discovered there was such a thing as archaeology, I just never looked back." (Interview, August 10, 1985)

Courtesy of Marie Wormington.

H. Marie Wormington, 1914–

"Artifacts themselves are not important—it's the information they can provide about cultures and about people." (Interview, August 10, 1985)

When the Depression intervened, Marie Wormington gave up her plans to study literature at the Sorbonne and entered the University of Denver, intending to study medicine or zoology. Inspired by E. B. Renaud, she switched to archaeology by her sophomore year and "never looked back." After graduation she began working on paleolithic sites in the Dordogne area of France and in 1935 she joined the staff of the Denver Museum of Natural History, where she became Curator of Archaeology for thirty-one years. Like other women archaeologists associated with museums, she devoted herself not only to the science of archaeology, but to making it meaningful to the nonprofessional.

Nationally and internationally recognized as a leader in the field of PaleoIndian or Early Man archaeology, Wormington's interest in the earliest peopling of North America began with the excavation of a small site in eastern Colorado in 1936. After publishing the pioneering study of PaleoIndian life, *Ancient Man in North America* (1939) and the classic text, *Prehistoric Indians of the Southwest* (1947), Wormington went back to school and received a Ph.D. from Radcliffe in 1954. She was the first to specialize in archaeology there and the second woman admitted to study in the Harvard anthropology department. At the same time, her excavations at Fremont village sites in southeastern Utah and her definitive monograph on Fremont culture initiated a reappraisal of Southwest prehistory. As an expert on the peopling of North America, Wormington has frequently represented the United States in international exchanges and was one of the first anthropologists to enter the Soviet Union and the People's Republic of China.

EDUCATION: B.A., anthropology, University of Denver, 1935; studied in France, England, Spain, 1935; M.A. 1950, Ph.D. 1953, anthropology, Radcliffe College.

FELLOWSHIPS AND AWARDS: Fanny Bullock Workman Fellowship, 1940–41; Alumni Award, University of Denver, 1952; Wenner-Gren Foundation Grants, 1952, 1958, 1969–70; Guggenheim Fellowship, 1970–71.

RESEARCH: Administers Colorado field schools for Denver Museum of Natural History, 1930–40s; archaeological research: France, 1935, paleolithic and archaic sites, 1940s–60s, southwestern Colorado, 1940s, western United States, 1936–68, Alberta, Canada, 1955–1956, USSR, Siberia, early man, 1958, Alaska, 1965; physical anthropology, Mexico, 1952; Pueblo pottery, 1950s.

PROFESSIONAL ACTIVITIES: Staff Archaeologist, 1935–37, Curator of Archaeology, 1937–68, Denver Museum of Natural History; Assistant Professor, University of Denver, 1947–49; Visiting Professor: University of Colorado, 1950–53, Arizona State University, 1968–69, Colorado College, 1969–70, University of Minnesota, 1973; Research Associate, University of Colorado Museum, 1968–86; Adjunct Professor, Colorado College, 1972–86; organizes Wenner-Gren conference on the role of museums in anthropology, 1954; Vice-President, 1950–51, 1955–56, President, 1968–69, SAA.

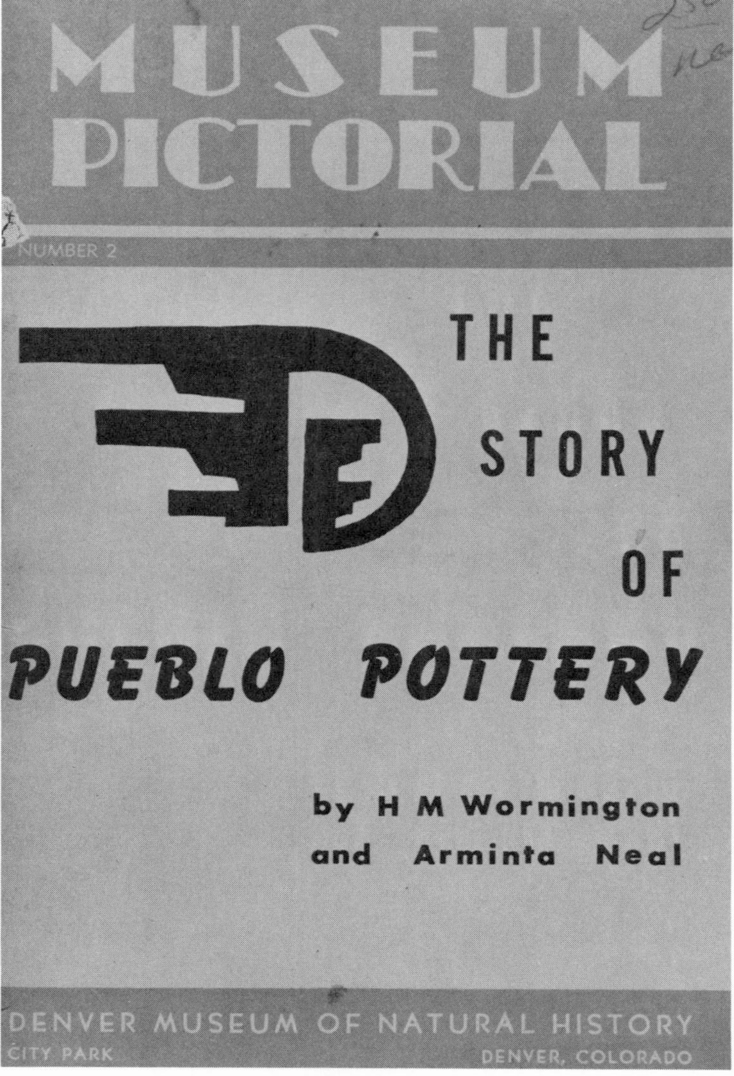

The Story of Pueblo Pottery (with Arminta Neal), Denver Museum of Natural History, Pictorial No. 2 (1951).

This publication is one of many in which Wormington synthesized anthropological knowledge and made it available to the layman. She used her initials in publishing because "the Director of the Denver Museum felt nobody would read a book written by a woman." (Interview, August 10, 1985)

Courtesy of the Denver Museum of Natural History. Photograph by Helga Teiwes. Courtesy of the Arizona State Museum.

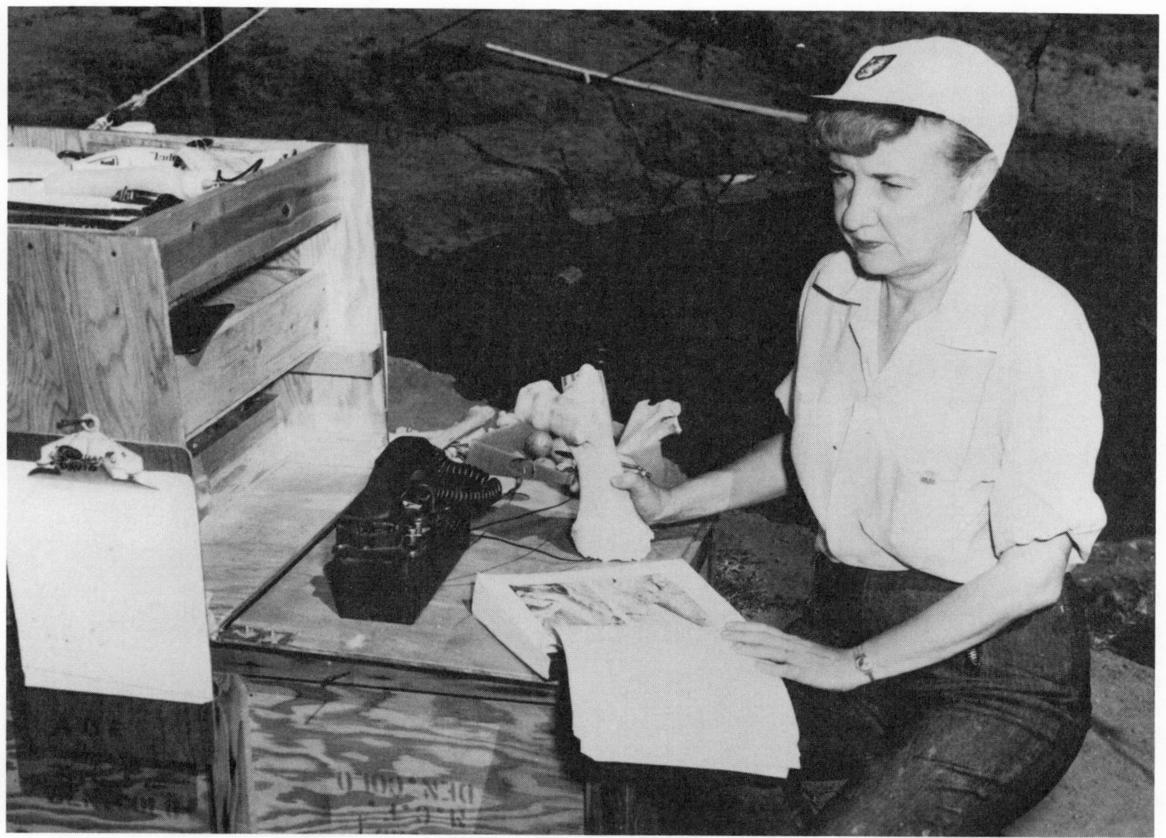

Marie Wormington examining bones at the Frazier Agate Basin PaleoIndian site, Weld County, Colorado, 1966.

"I think it is very important for a public who is interested in archaeology to have it available. It can offer a great deal—an understanding of what the human race is all about." (Interview, August 10, 1985)

Courtesy of the Denver Museum of Natural History.

Nathalie Woodbury analyzing pottery at the Museum of Northern Arizona, 1963.

In 1955, Nathalie and Richard Woodbury and Watson Smith reanalyzed the materials collected by Frederick Hodge at Hawikuh. These materials told much about Zuni prehistory and history.

Courtesy of the Museum of Northern Arizona.

NATHALIE WOODBURY, 1918–

"What I really like is problem-solving, and action, and editing, and administering things." (Interview, July 7, 1985)

Nathalie Woodbury's decision to be an anthropologist was "fostered by *Natural History Magazine*" and reinforced by studies at Barnard with Gladys Reichard. She was especially interested in archaeology and ethnology, "going back and forth between the two." (Interview, July 7, 1985) With her husband, Richard, and Watson Smith, she combined these interests when she restudied Zuni pottery from Hawikuh.

Woodbury's research in linguistics, ethnography, and archaeology has made her uniquely qualified for a lifetime of service to the discipline. She has held the elected offices of secretary, editor, historian, and board member for the American Anthropological Association, treasurer for the Society for American Archaeology, and secretary and councillor for the American Ethnological Society. In these positions, Woodbury has worked "to preserve the unity of anthropology while recognizing the uniqueness of each subfield's contribution." (Interview, July 7, 1985)

EDUCATION: A.B., anthropology, Barnard College, 1939; graduate work, ABD, anthropology, Columbia University, 1939–42.

FELLOWSHIPS AND AWARDS: Wenner-Gren Foundation Grant, AAA, 1969–70; AAA Distinguished Service Award, 1978; SAA 50th Anniversary Award for Outstanding Contributions to American Archaeology, 1985.

RESEARCH: Pueblo archaeology, 1938, 1939, 1953–56; Comanche ethnolinguistics, 1940; folklore, Bengali seamen, New York City, 1943–44; Mayan archaeology, contemporary crafts, 1947–48; Adena archaeology, 1950–51; Papago land use, 1961; Hawikuh archaeology, 1960s.

PROFESSIONAL ACTIVITIES: Instructor, Brooklyn College, 1944–45; Assistant Professor, Eastern New Mexico College, 1945–46; Instructor, University of Arizona, 1946–47; Assistant Archaeologist, Zacule Project, United Fruit Company, Guatemala, 1948–50; Instructor, 1952–58, Chair, 1954–56; Assistant Dean, 1956–58, Barnard College; Research Associate, Museum of Northern Arizona, 1958–66; Research Associate, Arizona State Museum, 1958–64; Co-editor, *Abstracts of New World Archaeology,* 1960–64; Research Associate, Smithsonian Institution, 1964–70; Research Associate, University of Massachusetts, 1970–71; Secretary, 1970–74, AAA Board, 1975–78; Associate Editor, *American Antiquity,* 1958–62, 1980–86; Editor, *Guide to Departments of Anthropology,* AAA, 1968–74; Editor, *Anthropology Newsletter* and *Bulletins,* AAA, 1968–76; Associate Editor, *American Anthropologist,* 1973–75; Column Editor, *Anthropology Newsletter,* 1979–present; Councillor, 1955–58, Secretary, 1960–66, AES; Treasurer, SAA, 1965–69.

Matsaki Polychrome ceramic jar. Matsaki, McKinley County, New Mexico. Protohistoric-historic Zuni, ca. 1475–1700. Collected by Nathalie and Richard Woodbury, 1953. Arizona State Museum Cat. No. 81–55–1.

"We did research in the Southwest in 1952 after getting to Columbia to teach. We were at El Morro National Monument. We dug two summers there. Nat and I were very much partners." (Richard Woodbury, Interview, July 7, 1985)

Photograph by Helga Teiwes. Courtesy of the Arizona State Museum.

Arts, Crafts, and Museums

Since the efforts of Alice Fletcher to establish the School of American Archaeology in Santa Fe, women have funded and organized Southwestern institutions, museums, and research projects. As traders, patrons, museum curators, and scholars they have played an important role in preserving, encouraging, and presenting Native American arts and crafts—yet another instance of concern with the expressive domain of culture being left to women.

Clara Lee Tanner examining baskets in the Arizona State Museum, ca. 1980.

"I've always had a terrific interest in art in general. I think it was rather natural that my interests in the Southwest would end up in native art." (Interview, September 24, 1985)

Courtesy of Clara Lee Tanner.

Clara Lee Tanner, 1905–

"I think that the Southwest itself has something you can't put your fingers on—it just is. And it is beautiful, and it is vast." (Interview, September 24, 1985)

Clara Lee Tanner grew up in Arizona and with her family often "visited ruins and Indian villages." "The anthropology bug" bit her when she took classes and field trips with Dean Byron Cummings. After graduating with one of the first M.A.s in archaeology from the University of Arizona, Tanner taught there for fifty years. Although she has given twenty-two different courses from classical archaeology to southwestern ethnology, she is best known for her courses in southwest Indian art. Developed in 1940, these courses are among the most popular ever taught at the University of Arizona.

Through public lectures and popular articles, Tanner has extended her teaching outside the university. "I decided early in the game that if anyone asked for a public lecture, I'd be glad to do it." "By conveying factual information in a straightforward manner," she has described to the non-anthropologists the "remarkable unbroken record" that characterizes southwest Indian arts and crafts. (Interview, September 24, 1985)

EDUCATION: B.A., 1927, M.A., 1928, archaeology, University of Arizona; postgraduate work at National University of Mexico, 1929, and Oriental Institute, University of Chicago, 1934.
AWARDS AND HONORS: 50th Anniversary Award of the Gallup Inter-Tribal Ceremonial Association, 1971; Arizona Press Women—Woman of the Year, 1971; Faculty Recognition Award, Tucson Trade Bureau, 1973; Faculty Achievement Award, University of Arizona Alumni Association, 1974; Sharlot Hall Award, 1985; Ph.D., University of Arizona, 1983.
RESEARCH: Archaeological fieldwork in northern Arizona, since 1930s; work in museums on archaeological and contemporary Indian arts and crafts, with specialization on easel art and basketry; fieldwork collecting from and interviewing Southwestern Indian artists.
PROFESSIONAL ACTIVITIES: Research Assistant, Arizona State Museum, 1924–27; Teaching Assistant, 1927–28, Instructor to Professor Emerita, 1928–85, University of Arizona; Editor, *The Kiva,* 1938–49; Assistant Professor, University of Denver, summer 1949; Judge at numerous Indian art shows; Contributor to professional and popular journals and newspapers; numerous public speaking activities.

Byron Cummings' 1930 summer field school at Ben Wetherill's ranch in northern Arizona. Standing left to right: Ben Shaw, Walter Olmsby, Byron Cummings. Seated left to right: Morris Burford, Mayme Burford, Clara Lee Tanner, Henrietta, Marie Gunst, Muriel Hann.

"Cummings had a breadth of vision and he instilled in students his great appreciation for Indians." (Interview, November 24, 1985)

Courtesy of the Arizona Historical Society.

(*facing page, top*) Worksheet for basket from the Hubbell Trading Post collection.

Tanner, noted authority on basketry, always felt that "facts were very important in the study of native peoples." (Interview, November 24, 1985)

Courtesy of Clara Lee Tanner. Photograph by Helga Teiwes. Courtesy of the Arizona State Museum.

(*facing page, bottom*) Apache basket jar, ca. 1900. Arizona State Museum, Cat. No. E-2815.

Before Tanner turned her attention to basketry, Helen Roberts and Mary Lois Kissel had finished major stylistic studies of Western Apache, Papago and Pima basketry.

Photograph by Helga Teiwes. Courtesy of the Arizona State Museum.

COLLECTION Hubbell Trading Po

BASKET NUMBER 3030
PROVENIENCE
DATE OF ACQUISITION

SHAPE: Tray X
Jar — Tus
Bowl

DIMENSIONS: Diameters: Rim 19 7/8
Base
Shoulder
Other

MATERIALS: Willow X
Martynia X
Yucca
Other

COLORS:

WEAVE: Coiled X — Wicker — Plaited

STITCHES: Per inch 11
Close — Even
Wide apart — Irregular
Quality of sewing good
long stitches, not too narrow

COILS: Per inch 4 1/2
Regular
Irregular

RIMS: Braided — Regular sewing X
Overcast — Other
All bl.

BEADS:

START: Plaiting — Knot
Coiled X — Wrapped

BOTTOM DESIGN in deep forms:
None
Present & style

DESIGN ANALYSIS:

a) Bl. center 5 coils
b) 1 wh coil
c) 6 outline "Apache" diamonds
d) 6 " " " out of c)
e) 6 " " " " " d)
horse in each (tail up.) w/cross above each
f). 6 triangles out of e) w/horse (tail up) in each + 2-row rectangle of alt bl/wh stitches to right exc. 1 to left.

Kate Peck Kent, 1979.

"Mrs. Kent is recognized by Southwestern archaeologists as the leading authority on the subject of prehistoric cotton textiles." (Letter from Harold S. Colton to American Philosophical Society, February 28, 1952)

Courtesy of the School of American Research.

Kate Peck Kent, 1914–1987

"Anthropology gives you a perspective that no other discipline gives you and a curiosity about other people." (Interview, September 4, 1985)

Kate Peck Kent became interested in archaeology because she "wanted to know what happened before European history." The enthusiasm for art and material culture instilled by Frederic Douglas at the Denver Art Museum was reinforced by graduate work at Columbia University with Gladys Reichard and Ralph Linton. "These were people who really thought that studying the arts and crafts of other people was important even though this was not mainstream anthropology." (Interview, September 4, 1985)

In 1937, Douglas asked Kent to analyze textile fragments from Tonto Ruins. Much of her fieldwork since then has been in museums and she has become well-known as a specialist in prehistoric and historic southwestern textiles. Believing that the anthropological perspective "that there are other ways of thinking besides our own" ought to be communicated, Kent has devoted much of her career to teaching. (Interview, September 4, 1985)

EDUCATION: B.A., anthropology, University of Denver, 1935; graduate studies, Columbia University, 1935–37, 1940–42; M.A., anthropology, University of Arizona, 1950.
FELLOWSHIPS AND AWARDS: Student Fellowship, Denver Art Museum, 1934–35; Resident Scholarship, Columbia University, 1935–36; F. H. Douglas grant, 1945–47, prehistoric textiles; APS Fellow, 1952, archaeological cotton; University of Denver International Relations Grant, 1966–67, 1969–70, Nigerian and Ghanan weavers' guilds; Weatherhead Resident Scholar, School of American Research, 1978–79; NEA grant for study of School of American Research southwestern textiles, 1980–83.
RESEARCH: Extensive museum work in historic and prehistoric Native American arts and industries, especially with textile technology; African ethnohistory and art, 1930s–86; Tonto textiles, 1937; Montezuma Castle textiles, 1940s; archaeology, late Pueblo-early Navajo sites, Gobernador area, 1941; Navajo weaving, 1956–86; historic Pueblo textiles, 1970s–1980s.
PROFESSIONAL ACTIVITIES: Graduate Assistant to Gladys Reichard, Barnard College, 1936–37; Assistant Curator of Indian Art, Denver Art Museum, 1937–38; Assistant, Museum of Northern Arizona, 1940; Curator of Native Arts, Denver Art Museum, 1942–44; Instructor to Associate Professor, 1950–78, Department Chair, 1973–78, University of Denver; Research Curator, School of American Research, 1979–80; Sr. Research Associate, Museum of International Folk Art, 1984–87.

Kent working on embroidered Pueblo dance kilts with Ramona Sakiestewa at the School of American Research, 1985.

"The whole research becomes more engrossing the more specimens I get hold of." (Letter to Katharine Bartlett, February 23, 1941)

Courtesy of the School of American Research.

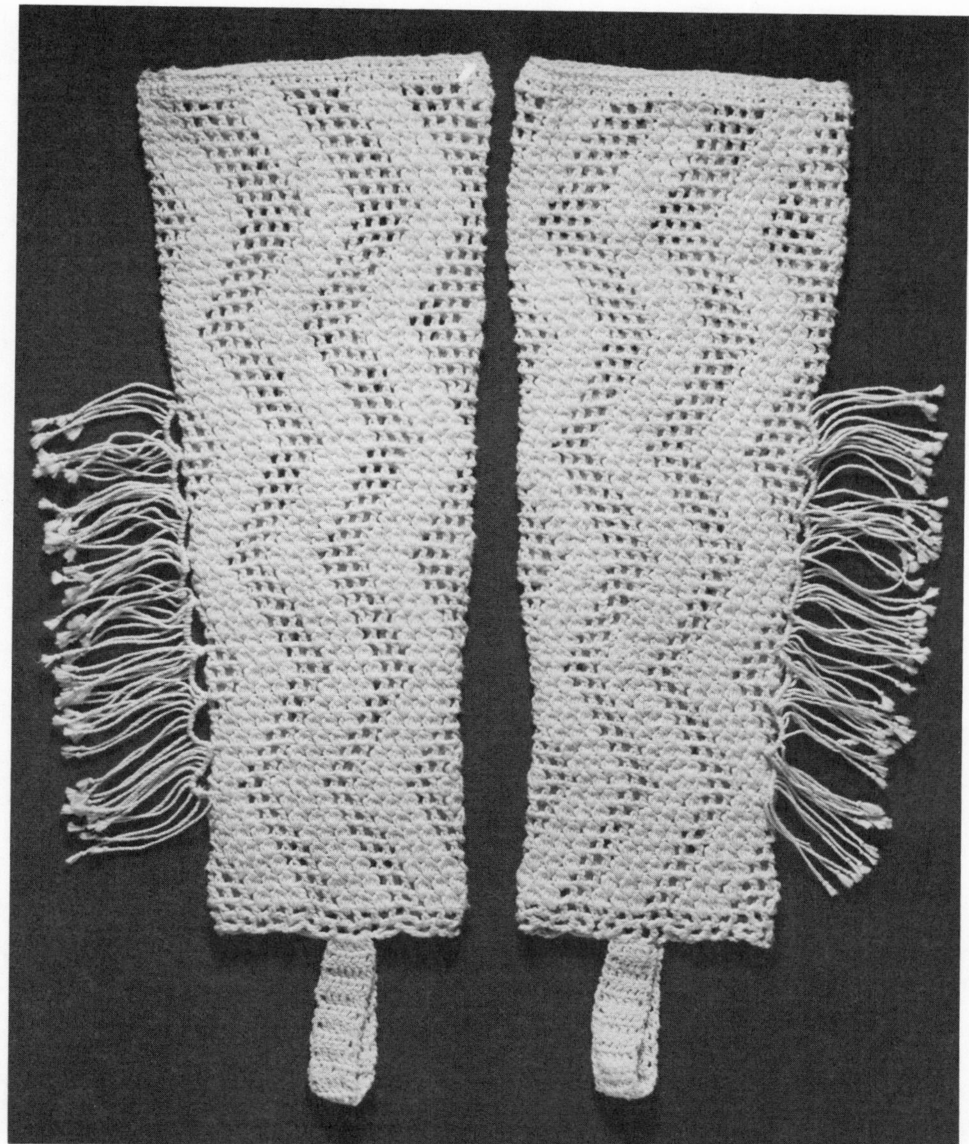

Crocheted leggings, San Juan Pueblo, 1969. Gift of Florence Hawley Ellis, Arizona State Museum Cat. No. E-8387.

Kate Peck Kent made extensive studies of Hopi knitting and crocheting. Her most recent books have been detailed studies of Pueblo and Navajo weaving techniques.

Photograph by Helga Teiwes. Courtesy of the Arizona State Museum.

Portrait of Mary-Russell Colton, ca. 1925.

"The next and following days at Lower Oraibi [in 1916], we saddled our mules and visited Second Mesa, saw the last snake dance ever given at Old Oraibi, and another snake dance at Hotevilla." (Harold S. Colton, "Reminiscences in Southwest Archaeology, IV," 1961).

Courtesy of Museum of Northern Arizona.

MARY-RUSSELL FERRELL COLTON, 1889–1971

"It is indeed, a happy thing to feel that others are aware of the work which we have carried on for so many years. I am very proud of my certificate from the Indian Arts and Crafts Board of the Department of the Interior." (Letter to René d'Harnoncourt, July 28, 1959)

In 1928, Harold S. and Mary-Russell Colton established the Museum of Northern Arizona in Flagstaff. They were joined in 1930 by Katharine Bartlett, a recent graduate in archaeology from the University of Denver. The Coltons and Bartlett formed a team that directed the museum's research on the Colorado Plateau in such diverse areas as archaeology, ethnology, zoology, botany and geology.

A well-known Philadelphia artist, Mary-Russell Colton sponsored the first exhibit of Arizona Indian crafts at the Arts and Crafts Guild in Philadelphia in 1925. As curator of art at the Museum of Northern Arizona, she carried on this tradition through the highly successful Hopi and Navajo Craftsmen Shows. Her only worry at the end of her career was "to find a young woman to train to take up my position and carry on the work among our Indian peoples." (Letter to René d'Harnoncourt, July 28, 1959)

EDUCATION: Private girls' schools in Pennsylvania; B.A., art, Philadelphia School of Design for Women, studies with Elliott Dangerfield and Henry B. Snell, 1907; graduate work at Philadelphia Academy of Art, 1908.

FELLOWSHIPS AND AWARDS: Pemberton Morris Prize for Pictorial Illustration, 1907; First Prize, Washington Water Color Club, 1918; Certificate of Appreciation, Indian Arts and Crafts Board, Department of Interior, 1960.

RESEARCH: Botanical field trips, British Columbia, 1908, 1910; exploratory field trips, Navajo and Hopi reservation, 1913, 1916, 1919, 1921, 1923, 1925; annual Museum of Northern Arizona collecting trips for Hopi and Navajo Craftsmen Shows, 1930–50.

PROFESSIONAL ACTIVITIES: Restorer of paintings, Missisippi, 1908–09; Professional artist in landscapes and portraits in watercolor and oil; Illustrator, with private studio in Philadelphia, 1909–26; Member of a group called The Ten Philadelphia Painters; exhibited regularly on East Coast and in Arizona, 1910–41; sponsored "Aboriginal American Craft, The Work of Indians of the Painted Desert of Arizona" exhibit at the Arts and Crafts Guild in Philadelphia, 1925; Co-founder, Museum of Northern Arizona, 1928; Curator of Art, Museum of Northern Arizona, 1928–50; designed ethnography and art exhibits, Museum of Northern Arizona, 1928–50; Founder and organizer of Hopi and Navajo Craftsmen Shows, Museum of Northern Arizona, 1930–50; Organizer of annual Arizona Arts and Crafts Shows, 1928–36; Chairman and Instructor, American Red Cross, 1942–46.

Colton painting at Flagstaff where she mixed ranch life with art in her studio in the woods, 1929.

In 1904, Colton was admitted to the Philadelphia School of Design for Women where she studied oil painting under Elliott Dangerfield and water color under Henry B. Snell. After five years of study she graduated with honors and opened a studio of her own.

Courtesy of the Museum of Northern Arizona.

"Navajo Shepherdess" by Mary-Russell Colton, 1918.

By 1908, Colton was an award-winning painter. Her interest in Indian art was an outgrowth of her interest in watercolor and oil painting.

Courtesy of the Museum of Northern Arizona.

Katherine Bartlett in the library at the Museum of Northern Arizona, 1979.

"I think that I really enjoyed the library almost more than any of the other things that I've ever done." (Interview, August 24, 1985)

Photograph by Middleton. Courtesy of the Museum of Northern Arizona.

Katharine Bartlett, 1907–

"I think the only continuous thing that I have really had an interest in was the Museum as a whole." (Interview, August 24, 1985)

Unable to attend Smith College for financial reasons, Denver native Katharine Bartlett went to the University of Denver where Renaud's courses "sold" her on anthropology. After she received her M.A. in 1930, Harold Colton offered her a summer job at the Museum of Northern Arizona taking care of materials coming in from an excavation east of Flagstaff. At the end of the summer, the Coltons asked her to stay on and to live in their house.

For twenty-five years, Bartlett lived and worked with the Coltons and did "just about everything you can think of in a museum." As curator of anthropology and archaeology, she did fieldwork and collecting in northern Arizona in addition to museum research. In the late 1940s, Bartlett took over the library as well and has become famous for helping southwestern scholars "find what they needed for their research projects." (Interview, August 24, 1985)

EDUCATION: B.A., 1929, M.A., 1930, anthropology, University of Denver.
FELLOWSHIPS AND AWARDS: Rockefeller Foundation Museum Internship to Brooklyn Museum to study museology, 1936–37.
RESEARCH: Archaeological fieldwork with Harold S. Colton in northern Arizona, 1930–50s; Museum of Northern Arizona archaeological survey and administration of site location files; ethnographic fieldwork with Hopi, 1930s–50s; meteorology, 1930s–40s; designs on Havasupai baskets, 1944; prehistoric osteology, 1944–55; history of Flagstaff, 1954–56.
PROFESSIONAL ACTIVITIES: Teaching Assistant, University of Denver, 1928–30; Curator of Anthropology and Archaeology, Museum of Northern Arizona, 1930–52; assists with Hopi and Navajo shows at Museum of Northern Arizona, 1930s–80s; judging at various Indian art shows; Secretary of the Social Science Section of Southwest Division of AAAS, 1942; editing, administration and public relations for Museum of Northern Arizona, 1940s–50s; Assistant Editor, *American Antiquity,* 1950–51; Curator of History and Librarian, Museum of Northern Arizona, 1953–75.

Judging Basketry at the Hopi Show, 1956. (*left to right*) Ned Danson, Jackie Turner, Mary-Russell Colton, Katharine Bartlett, Jan Danson, David Breternitz.

One of Colton's main concerns was the encouragement of Native American art. The Museum of Northern Arizona began sponsoring the Hopi Craftsman Show in 1930 and the Navajo Craftsman Show in 1942. Colton and Bartlett personally selected all pieces shown in the show.

Photograph by Turner. Courtesy of the Museum of Northern Arizona.

Program, Hopi Craftsman Show, Museum of Northern Arizona, 1939.

"I was a jack-of-all-trades. In the beginning there were so few people and we really all did everything. We had to stop what we were doing and all help put up an exhibition." (Interview, August 24, 1985)

Katharine Bartlett, Mary-Russell Colton, and Harold Colton on lac collecting trip, October 26, 1942.

The Museum of Northern Arizona truck was a common sight all over the Colorado Plateau. "I came here to spend a summer and I've been here ever since." (Interview, August 24, 1985)

Courtesy of the Museum of Northern Arizona.

Mary Cabot Wheelwright in her library, Northeast Harbour, Maine, 1912.

"My only qualifications for the undertaking are plenty of time and patience, some knowledge of other religions and backgrounds, and a respect and love for the Navajo people." (Wheelwright Museum Archives)

Photograph by Florence Maynard. Courtesy of the Wheelwright Museum of the American Indian.

Mary Cabot Wheelwright, 1878–1958

"I felt so definitely that I wanted my museum to be different from the usual museum." (Wheelwright Museum Archives)

Wealthy Bostonian Mary Cabot Wheelwright "became interested in Navajo religion while on a horseback trip on the Navajo reservation in 1926." For over twenty years, she spent part of every spring and autumn at Newcomb's Trading Post. There she met Hosteen Klah who asked her to record myths, prayers, songs, and sandpaintings "so that they would not be lost forever." In 1927 Wheelwright began to record Klah's Nightway songs. Ten years later she built the Museum of Navajo Ceremonial Art in the shape of a ceremonial hogan to provide a home for these collections. (Wheelwright Museum Archives)

Like Parsons, Wheelwright revolted against her upperclass Eastern background and used her inheritance in the interests of southwestern anthropology. Wheelwright had no formal training, but had an instinctive feeling for what ought to be done and the energy and means to see that it was done. Before her death, the Navajo people thanked her for "building the things of the spirit into visible and physical form in the Museum of Navajo Ceremonial Art." (Paul Jones, Navajo Tribal Chairman, *The New Mexican*, December 4, 1956)

EDUCATION: No formal education, attended finishing school and studied with private tutors in Boston.

RESEARCH: Annual trips to Navajo reservation after 1926 to record Navajo ceremonies and songs; India to search for symbols comparable to Navajo rites, 1940.

PROFESSIONAL ACTIVITIES: Social and civic work in Boston, including founding of South End Music School, 1912–1917; founded The Carry-On Shop, Boston, 1912–1925; owner, Indian arts and crafts store in New York City; arranged Indian art and Hispanic art exhibits, 1920s–40s; Founder and Director, Museum of Navajo Ceremonial Art, 1937–58.

Mary Wheelwright with Hosteen Klah at her home in Maine, ca. 1930.

Both Mary Wheelwright and Franc Newcomb worked closely with Hosteen Klah, a Navajo singer, sandpainter, sheepherder, and weaver, who "had such gentleness and such power." Newcomb has said that "I think Mary's book is a sort of a monument to Klah." (Letter to Gladys Reichard, January 30, 1938)

Courtesy of the Wheelwright Museum of the American Indian.

Hosteen Klah (Ty'aai), ca. 1935.

Klah considered both Wheelwright and Newcomb his apprentices. "I have pleasant memories of long winter evenings before the huge open fireplace, sometimes with a baby on my lap or perhaps with my hands busy sewing some small garment while I listened to the deep voice of Hosteen Klah recounting traditions of his people or tribal events that took place long before he was born." (Newcomb, *Hosteen Klah*, 1964)

Photograph by T. Harmon Parkhurst. Courtesy of the Museum of New Mexico.

Navajo belt buckle, pre-1940. Gift of Mary Cabot Wheelwright, Arizona State Museum, Cat. No. E-1242.

Wheelwright was a major collector of Indian art. She opened a store in Boston in order to introduce southwestern art to Easterners. She also "financed trader Cozy McSparron's attempts to improve Navajo weaving" in the Chinle area in the 1930s and 1940s. (Sallie Wagner, Interview, July 30, 1986)

Photograph by Helga Teiwes. Courtesy of the Arizona State Museum.

Millicent Rogers, 1946.

Photograph by Louise Dahl-Wolfe. Courtesy of the Millicent Rogers Museum, Taos, New Mexico.

Millicent Rogers, 1902–1953

"She had a way of transforming the mundane into something interesting, refined, and above all personal." (George Headley, quoted in Neil Letson, "A Woman of Some Importance," 1984)

A wealthy New Yorker of "unassailable taste," Millicent Rogers was born into a very different world from the Southwest Indian cultures that she came to love. The granddaughter of Henry Huttleston Rogers, "the hell hound of Wall Street," she grew up on large estates and in rented castles, surrounded by the social and cultural elite of the age. "From her mother she inherited a flair for beautiful clothes; she had her father's restless energy and his pragmatic approach to money." Unlike many heiresses, she had a keen intelligence "accompanied by artistic and literary sensibility." (Neil Letson, "A Woman of Some Importance," 1984)

Rogers first visted New Mexico in 1947 and the discovery of Taos changed her life. She collected Indian jewelry with great discernment, learned Navajo and Pueblo silversmithing techniques, and adapted southwestern designs to the jewelry she herself designed at "Turtlewalk," her Taos home. As J. Watson Webb, Jr., remarked, "whatever interested her . . . became an assembly of the very best of its kind." (Neil Letson, "A Woman of Some Importance," 1984) The Southwest Indian textiles and jewelry she collected in the 1940s became the center of the Millicent Rogers Museum, founded in Taos in 1953 in her memory. The museum has grown into an important cultural center and repository of Navajo, Pueblo, and Hispanic arts that epitomizes her highly distinctive style.

EDUCATION: Tutors and small private schools in New York City and Washington, D.C.

RESEARCH: First came to Taos in June, 1947 and between then and her death in 1953 amassed 2,000 pieces of Navajo and Pueblo art, including one of the best collections of Native American jewelry in the world. Also researched and learned Navajo and Pueblo metalsmithing techniques. Serious work as a jeweler 1940s ff.

PROFESSIONAL ACTIVITIES: Exhibit (with Charles James): "A Decade of Design," Brooklyn Museum, 1948.

Millicent Rogers in her kitchen, dressed in Southwest Indian-style clothes and dyeing velvet.

"It is for her clothes that Millicent is most often remembered. She had an extraordinary flair for them and the lean, tall figure to wear anything." (Neil Letson, "A Woman of Some Importance," 1984)

Courtesy of the Millicent Rogers Museum, Taos, New Mexico.

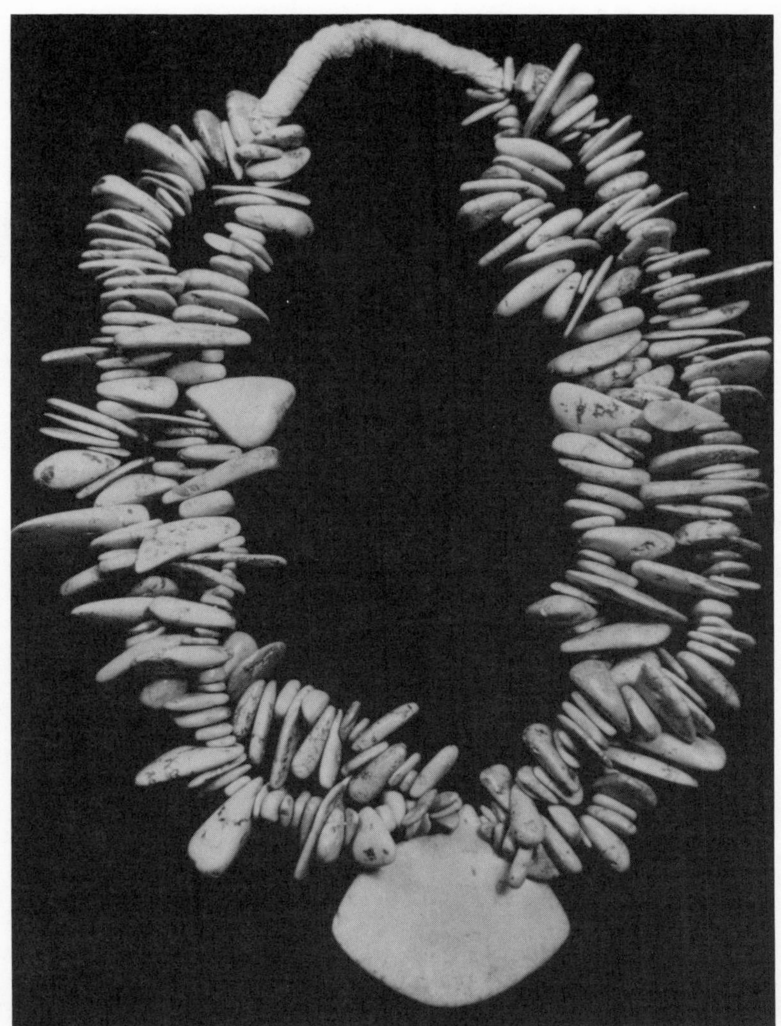

Turquoise tab necklace by Leekya Deyuse, Zuni Pueblo, ca. 1940.

Originally purchased by Millicent Rogers at the Gallup Inter-Tribal Ceremonial in 1947, this necklace by Zuni Pueblo's most famous stone carver consists of a double strand of large Cerrillos blue gem turquoise tabs weighing almost four pounds. "She was one of three or four collectors who had the vision and conviction to gather Southwest Indian material during the 1940s and 1950s—pieces representative, distinctive, and not to be found today." (Neil Letson, "A Woman of Some Importance," 1984)

Courtesy of the Millicent Rogers Museum, Taos, New Mexico.

Pablita Velarde, ca. 1965.

"She thought of how she herself had often gone alone to the mountains and found peace there, feeling near to the Great One as she listened to the mountain's breath-sound." (*Old Father, the Storyteller,* 1960)

Courtesy of the Museum of New Mexico.

Pablita Velarde, 1918–

"I was one of the fortunate children of my generation who were probably the last to hear stories firsthand from Great-grandfather or Grandfather. I treasure that memory and I have tried to preserve it." (*Old Father, the Storyteller,* 1960)

Native American women have spoken eloquently for themselves in both traditional and non-traditional art forms. The art of Santa Clara painter Pablita Velarde is a unique and compelling expression of Pueblo experience. First introduced to easel art by Tonita Peña, Pablita Velarde studied with Dorothy Dunn in the early 1930s at Santa Fe's Indian School. She soon developed a style that Dunn later described as embodying "the poise and gentle strength of a Pueblo woman." ("Pablita Velarde, Painter of Pueblo Life," 1952)

A portrait of a Santa Clara potter shaping a large storage jar was the first of countless oil and watercolor paintings depicting Pueblo crafts, social organization, ceremonies, and individuals. Her earth paintings represent myths, supernatural beings and legends handed down from her ancestors. Velarde sees great beauty in "yesterday" and says she cannot contribute thoughts of value unless she appreciates and understands the past (Marion E. Gridley, ed., *Indians of Today,* 1971).

Pablita Velarde has also written and illustrated a book of Pueblo legends, *Old Father, the Story Teller,* because she "thought it would be a good thing if an Indian wrote an Indian book." (*Old Father, the Storyteller,* 1960)

EDUCATION: High School Diploma, U.S. Indian School, Santa Fe, 1936; studied painting with Dorothy Dunn.

FELLOWSHIPS AND AWARDS: Prizes from Philbrook Art Center, Gallup Ceremonial and other juried shows; Philbrook Grand Purchase Prize, 1953; Grand Prizes, Gallup Ceremonial, 1955–1959; France's Palmes d'Academiques, 1954; voted one of Best Western Books, 1961.

PROFESSIONAL ACTIVITIES: Teacher's assistant, Santa Clara Day School, 1936–38; tours midwest with Ernest Thompson Seton and family, 1938; painter with private studio at Santa Clara, 1938–85, and Albuquerque, 1949–85; commission work on murals includes: Bandelier National Monument, 1939–48; Maisel Building, Albuquerque, 1939–40; Foote Cafeteria, Houston, 1957; Western Skies Hotel, Albuquerque, 1958; WPA art projects, 1934; exhibits at numerous museums beginning with Chicago Century of Progress, 1933; numerous painting demonstrations; illustrator of books.

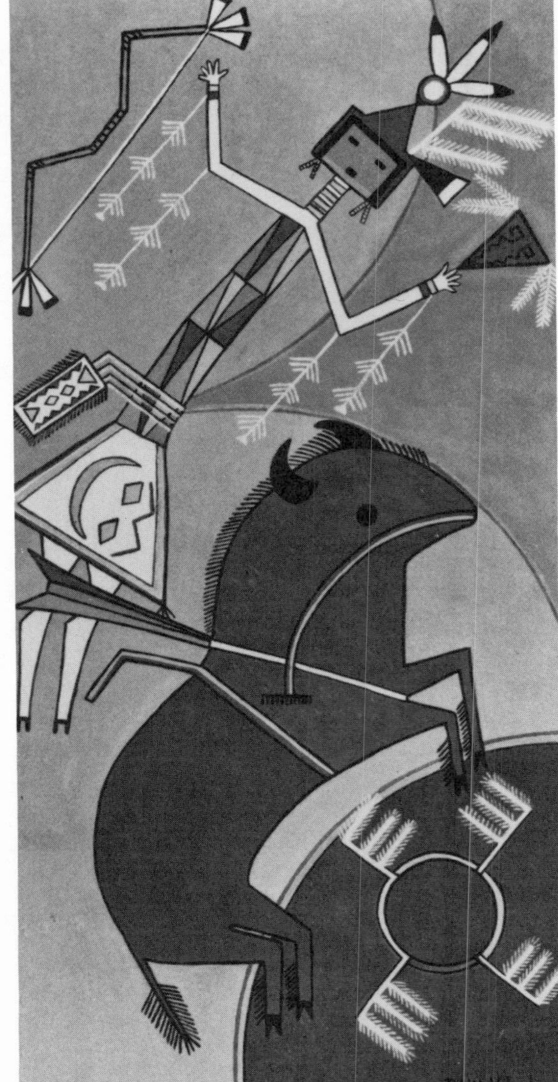

"Buffalo Who Never Dies" by Pablita Velarde, 1962. Arizona State Museum, Cat. No. L-132.

Earth painting based on the Navajo sandpainting "Holy People overcome Buffalo" from Male Shootingway. "When Scavenger Boy killed the last buffalo, it brought hunger and hardship to many people. Rainbow Lady offered her own spirit to be placed in buffalo. The great Yei accepted and the buffalo came back to life." (Painting notes, 1962, Arizona State Museum catalogue cards)

Photograph by Helga Teiwes. Courtesy of the Arizona State Museum.

Photography

In addition to women scholars studying Native American artists and arts, many Anglo women artists have devoted their skills to portraying southwestern Indian cultures in a variety of media.

As the emphasis in the photographic documentation of Native Americans shifted from contrived studio portraits to ethnographic realism, and as photographic equipment became more manageable and useable in the field, women soon distinguished themselves as honest and sensitive interpreters of the everyday life of southwestern Indians.

Laura Gilpin, 1978.

"I haven't been after any reputation. If you're going to work with people the way I do, why, you want to do it just as quietly as possible." (Quoted in David Vestal, "Laura Gilpin: Photographer of the Southwest," 1977)

Photograph by John Schaefer. Courtesy of the Center for Creative Photography, University of Arizona.

Laura Gilpin, 1891–1979

"It is the kind of photography that can't be done in a hurry; you have to be trusted." (Quoted in Terence R. Pitts, "The Early Work of Laura Gilpin, 1917–1932," 1981)

In the past seventy-five years, Laura Gilpin has come to be recognized as the foremost photographer of southwestern Native Americans. After graduating from New York's Clarence H. White School of Photography in 1917, she came to the Southwest and concentrated on panoramic landscapes. Her interest in the landscape evolved into photographic essays on the archaeological ruins and indigenous inhabitants of Arizona and New Mexico. As Vicki Goldberg, among others, has remarked, "few women in the history of photography have so dedicated themselves to the landscape." ("An Eye for Ageless Beauty," 1986)

In 1930, Gilpin accompanied Elizabeth Forster to the Navajo Reservation where she was shocked by their poverty and awed by their dignity. She spent several decades with the Navajo, and in 1968 her sensitive photographs of their daily life and relationship with the land were published in *The Enduring Navaho,* which she described as "an interpretation of a wonderful people just as I have found them, a people having great pride, dignity, and ability who deserve our sincere respect."

EDUCATION: Diploma, Clarence H. White School of Photography, 1917; postgraduate work, White School of Photography, 1917–18.

FELLOWSHIPS AND AWARDS: Certificate of Appreciation, Indian Arts and Crafts Board, 1967; Western Heritage Award, 1968; Citation, Photographers of Southwest, 1971; First Annual Governor's Award, New Mexico Arts Commission, 1974; Fellow, School of American Research, 1971; Guggenheim Fellowship, 1975, to work on hand-coated platinum papers; Honorary D.Lit., University of New Mexico, 1970; Honorary Ph.D., Colorado College, 1979

RESEARCH: In Southwest, 1920–70s; Europe, 1922; numerous trips to archaeological ruins, 1920s–1960s; to Navajo, 1930–31, 1948–68; Rio Grande Pueblos, 1920s–30s; Canyon de Chelly project, 1968–79; Yucatan, 1932, 1946.

PROFESSIONAL ACTIVITIES: Freelance and commercial photographer—studios in New York City, 1918–21, in Colorado, 1918–45, in Santa Fe, 1945–79; Instructor in Photography, Chappell School of Art, Denver, 1926–30; Colorado Springs Fine Art Center, 1930, 1940–41; worked on WPA guides, 1930s; Photographer for Central City Theatre, University of Colorado, 1932–36; Public relations photographer, Boeing Airplane Company, Wichita, Kansas, 1942–45; numerous group and private shows, 1922–1985; Retrospective show, Museum of New Mexico, 1974; Chairman, Indian Arts Fund, 1958.

Laura Gilpin at work in 1971.

Ansel Adams described Gilpin as "one of the most important photographers of our time who seems never to have faltered in her desire to record the earth and people around her." (Quoted in Turner Browne, *MacMillan Biographical Encyclopedia of Photographic Artists and Innovators,* 1983)

Photograph by Fred Mang, Jr., © 1971. Courtesy of the Amon Carter Museum and Fred Mang, Jr.

Navaho Ethel Kellerwood, n.d.

"I had just started out to photograph ruins. I was scared to death of the people. I didn't do too much with the people for a long while, 'til I got to know them. You can't do it in a hurry." (Quoted in David Vestal, "Laura Gilpin, Photographer of the Southwest," 1977)

Photograph by Laura Gilpin. Courtesy of the Center for Creative Photography, University of Arizona and Amon Carter Museum.

Round Tower, Cliff Palace, Mesa Verde, Colorado, 1925.

After hearing an archaeologist's lecture on Teotihuacan with very "poor" slides, Gilpin wondered "why in the world can't archaeologists and a photographer get together? So I couldn't go to Mexico, but I could get to Mesa Verde, and I did a lot of work there in the early days." (Quoted in David Vestal, "Laura Gilpin, Photographer of the Southwest," 1977) Gilpin first visited Mesa Verde in 1924 and subsequently published a slide lecture and guidebook. *The Mesa Verde National Park* (1927) set a precedent of doing the research, writing, and design as well as the photography that she would follow in all her later books.

Photograph by Laura Gilpin, © 1981. Courtesy of Laura Gilpin Collection, Amon Carter Museum.

Elizabeth Hegemann in front of Shonto Trading Post, 1934. (*A Collection of Photographs of the Navajo and Hopi Country,* 1961)

After their marriage in 1929, Elizabeth and Harry Rorick acquired and very successfully operated the isolated Shonto Trading Post.

Courtesy of the University of New Mexico Press.

Elizabeth Hegemann, 1897–1962

"My only thought was to catch a true reflection of Reservation life around me during the years I lived among the Navajos and Hopis." (*Navajo Trading Days,* 1963)

Traders who live on reservations have opportunities and experiences that scholars are rarely afforded in a few months of summer research. In the 1920s and 1930s, Elizabeth Hegemann lived as a trader at Shonto Trading Post and at the Grand Canyon as the wife of a National Park Service official. She used her "postcard-sized" Kodak camera over 800 times to record Native American life, the landscape on the Colorado Plateau, and life around the Grand Canyon.

Hegemann saw her photographs as a historical record and made no attempt to retouch or disguise flaws. Like the text of her book *Navaho Trading Days* (1963), they are personal documents and recollections rather than scholarly studies. Hegemann regarded photography as one of the best media to promote better understanding of the region and of Navajo and Hopi ways of life.

EDUCATION: Attended Miss Doherty's College Preparatory School in Cincinnati, 1915.
RESEARCH: Annual trips to Grand Canyon, 1910–1925; travel throughout Navajo, Hopi, Havasupai, and Walapai lands taking nonprofessional photographs, 1920s–30s.
PROFESSIONAL ACTIVITIES: Trader, Tuba City, 1928–29; Trader, Shonto Trading Post, 1929–39; Photographer of Navajo and Hopi life, 1920s–30s; Exhibit of photographs, 1961.

Navajo mother and child, Paiute Canyon, 1928.

"On the high ridge between Paiute and Navaho canyons, this Navajo woman waits by the pile of cedar posts her husband has cut for a trader." (*Navajo Trading Days*, 1963)

Photograph by Elizabeth Hegemann. Courtesy of the University of New Mexico Press.

Main road to Acoma Pueblo, 1928.

"The camera I used for most of these photographs was an old Eastman postcard-size Kodak, although I did take some after 1928 with a small Graflex." (*A Collection of Photographs of the Navajo and Hopi Country, 1922–1932*, 1961)

Photograph by Elizabeth Hegemann. Courtesy of the Arizona State Museum.

Helga Teiwes photographing site features at Snaketown, Pima Reservation, Arizona, 1965.

"Helga . . . brought to the task of photo-recording a talent rarely found in archaeological endeavours. Despite the fact that this was her first field assignment, she quickly mastered the light, angle, subject matter, and physical problems to provide consistently excellent results." (Emil Haury, *The Hohokam,* 1976)

Photograph by James Scicenti. Courtesy of the Arizona State Museum.

HELGA TEIWES, 1930–

"Photography is a tool to observe people, their culture, and their environment, and gain respect and understanding for them and ourselves." (Letter to Barbara Babcock and Nancy Parezo, December, 1985)

Helga Teiwes was born and educated in Germany. After immigrating to the United States in 1960, she worked for several years as a commercial photographer. In 1964 she was hired as field photographer for the Snaketown excavations under the direction of Emil Haury. She has been staff photographer for the Arizona State Museum since then.

Specializing in ethnographic photography, Teiwes has traveled extensively throughout the Greater Southwest with museum curators documenting daily and ceremonial life. Her work with the Papago, Tarahumara, and Hopi is widely known and admired.

In addition to her still photography, Teiwes has produced two documentary color films, *Excavations at Snaketown* (1967) and *Mission San Xavier del Bac* (1969).

EDUCATION: M.A., photography, Hehmke-Winderer Studio, Dusseldorf, Germany, 1957; B.A., art history, University of Arizona, 1978.

FELLOWSHIPS AND AWARDS: University of Arizona Foundation Grant to document life of Papago Indians, 1977; Grand Prize in the photography contest of the World Photography Society, Capitola, CA, 1984; Industrial Photography Magazine Award, 1985.

RESEARCH: Extensive photographic trips in Southwest, northern Mexico, and western United States.

PROFESSIONAL ACTIVITIES: Commercial Photographer and Instructor, Hehmke-Winterer Studio, 1950–57; Staff Photographer, Bagel Printing Company, 1957–60; Immigrated to US, 1960; Staff Photographer, Brodatz Custom Lab and Cartiers, 1960–62; Commercial Photographer and Color Transparency Retoucher, CCF Color Lab, New York City, 1962–64; Field Photographer, Snaketown excavations, 1964–65; Photographer, Arizona State Museum, 1965–87; photography and production of two documentary films on Snaketown and Mission San Xavier del Bac; Photographic Exhibit, "Hopi Harvest," Arizona State Museum, 1983; Photographic exhibit "Hopi Harvest" sponsored by the Arizona Commission of the Arts as a travelling exhibit, 1986; taught photographic techniques in numerous seminars and workshops; Member, Professional Photographers of America; photographs used in numerous anthropological articles and books.

Apache Puberty Ceremony, San Carlos Indian Reservation, 1981.

Linette Anderson dances in a kneeling position. This segment of the ceremony is a re-creation of the impregnation of Changing Woman by the sun.

Photograph by Helga Teiwes. Courtesy of the Arizona State Museum.

Nancy Wood, ca. 1979

"For me there is no separation between the exotic life I live as a woman and the exotic life I live as an artist." (Letter to Bruce Hilpert, 1986)

Courtesy of Nancy Wood.

Nancy Wood, 1936–

> "Honesty in photography, as honesty in life, is the hardest thing of all. It requires discipline, observation, painstaking work." (Letter to Bruce Hilpert, 1986)

Nancy Wood is a professional photographer, writer, poet, and musician. After years spent documenting Native American and American life in Colorado, she has begun to make a historical record of everyday experience at Taos Pueblo. "Drawing from more than 20 years of experience with these Indians, I have begun to examine their relationship to nature, to tradition, to village life, and to each other." It will take Wood until 1989 to complete the study that already involves more than 20,000 negatives and hundreds of hours of oral histories.

Nancy Wood "does not look at photography so much as an art form, but as a means of communication." The challenge for her is "to discover validity in every situation, to see beauty in the mundane." (Letter to Bruce Hilpert, 1986)

EDUCATION: Bucknell College; University of Colorado; studied with Roy Stryker.
FELLOWSHIPS AND AWARDS: Colorado Council on the Arts and Humanities Grant, 1975; Colorado Centennial Commission Grant, 1976; Colorado State Historical Society Grant, 1977; Colorado Council on the Arts and Humanities: Art in Public Places Program Grant, 1981; The Maytag Foundation Grant, 1984; Border Regional Library Association Award, 1975; nominated for Pulitzer Prize in music, 1977.
RESEARCH: Studies and photographs Utes, 1975–80; Taos Pueblo, 1984–86.
PROFESSIONAL ACTIVITIES: Professional photographer and freelance writer; production of 60-minute documentary film, "Cowboys" for *The Bill Moyers Journal*, PBS, 1974; publications of photographs, fiction, and poetry in numerous magazines including *Audubon, McCall's, American Heritage, Time, Empire.*

Mrs. Romero, Taos Pueblo.

Photograph by and courtesy of Nancy Wood, 1985.

"These photographs of Taos Pueblo women represent the spirit of Taos Pueblo. In these women I find strength, compassion, stoicism; a richness of spirit that makes you say, yes, they may be poor, their lives hard, their culture in the midst of drastic change, but you know that for a thousand years they have been the glue that has held the pueblo together. May they endure for a thousand more." (Letter to Bruce Hilpert, 1986)

Mrs. Sandoval, Taos Pueblo.

Photograph by and courtesy of Nancy Wood, 1985.

Novelists, Poets, and Popularizers

To women has fallen the important task of translating anthropological research to the general public in both words and images. This has taken many forms—from writing novels and children's books to lobbying for Indian rights and arranging "detours" through "Indian Country." Alice Marriott, Erna Fergusson, Mary Austin, Mary Colter, and Laura Armer are but five of the countless women novelists, essayists, poets, and painters who influentially interpreted southwestern Indian life to the American public.

Mary Austin, ca. 1900, at the beginning of her writing career, photographed by mentor Charles Lummis and wearing his Stetson.

"By Land, I mean all those things common to a given region. . . . the flow of prevailing winds, the succession of vegetal cover, the legend of ancient life, and the scene, above everything the magnificently shaped and colored scene." (*The Land of Journey's Ending,* 1924)

Courtesy of the Southwest Museum.

Mary Austin, 1868–1934

"... what passed between me and the Land ... has not, perhaps never could, come into being with anybody else." (Quoted in Augusta Fink, *I-Mary,* 1983)

Feminist author and naturalist Mary Austin began her literary career in California and first visited the Southwest in 1917. Her many publications expressed Austin's passionate identification with the land and her outrage against the mistreatment of its native inhabitants and the misuse of women's gifts.

Austin concentrated her diverse talents on the Southwest while building a home in Santa Fe in the 1920s. At Mabel Dodge Luhan's request, she joined the fight against the Bursum Bill and campaigned successfully for Pueblo land and water rights. Austin also gave generously of her time and money to the Indian Arts Fund established to encourage traditional Pueblo art. The landscape and peoples of Arizona and New Mexico inspired her popular work *The Land of Journey's Ending* (1924), and *Taos Pueblo* (1930), her collaboration with photographer Ansel Adams.

EDUCATION: B.A., English, education, Blackburn College, 1888.

FELLOWSHIPS AND AWARDS: LL.D., University of New Mexico, 1933.

RESEARCH: Owens Valley Paiute, 1893–99; Paiute women, George's Creek, CA.; Paiute "campoody" near Bishop, California, religion, 1895–99; lived and worked in Southwest, 1917–34.

PROFESSIONAL ACTIVITIES: Teacher, Inyo Academy, Bishop, California, 1895; Teacher, Lone Pine, 1897; Teacher, Normal School, Los Angeles, 1899; involved with both suffrage and labor movements, 1911; lectures at many institutions including University of California–Berkeley, Yale University, Southwest Museum, 1917ff.; Associate in Native American Literature, School of American Research, 1918; lobbied against Bursum Bill, 1922–23; Member, Indian Arts Fund, 1925; Organizer, Old Santa Fe Association, 1925; Ministry of Education seminar in Mexico on Indian art and culture, 1930; fund-raising, New Mexico Association on Indian Affairs, 1930; raised funds to save El Santuario at Chimayo, 1929; with Frank and Alta Applegate, organized movement to support Spanish-colonial arts, c. 1927.

(*above*) Daniel T. MacDougal and Austin using a device for measuring tree growth in Tucson, 1923.

Austin's introduction to Papagueria in 1919 by MacDougal inspired *The Land of Journey's Ending*. "I have been enough in the Southwest to understand that what would come to me there would be immensely more radiant and splendid than what came in California." (Letter to MacDougal, July 5, 1920)

Courtesy of the Arizona Historical Society.

(*left*) Cover, *Indian Pottery of the Rio Grande,* 1934.

In her efforts to preserve and encourage Pueblo art, Mary Austin wrote this useful guide in which she perceptively observed: "Design is for them a language which is related itself to the processes they conceive of as going on in all nature and all created things . . . to go to the river for water with an ugly jar is the gravest impertinence." (*Indian Pottery of the Rio Grande,* 1934)

Courtesy of Special Collections, University of Arizona. Photograph by Helga Teiwes. Courtesy of the Arizona State Museum.

South House, Woman Winnowing Grain, Taos Pueblo, New Mexico, ca. 1929.

In her text which accompanied Ansel Adams' photographs of Taos Pueblo, Mary Austin remarked, "There is another sort of beauty playing always about the Pueblo country, beauty of cloud and rain and split sunlight . . . Everywhere peace, impenetrable timelessness of peace, as though the pueblo and all it contains were shut in a glassy fourth dimension, near and at the same time inaccessibly remote." (*Taos Pueblo,* 1930)

Photograph by Ansel Adams. Courtesy of the Trustees of the Ansel Adams Publishing Rights Trust.

Laura Adams Armer, 1932.

"Here with the Navajos, I am not hampered by trivialities, but I have learned that one must win his own place in the spiritual world, painfully and alone." (*In Navajo Land,* 1962)

Drawing by Constance Narr. (*New York Herald Tribune,* May 1, 1932) Photograph by Helga Teiwes. Courtesy of the Arizona State Museum.

Laura Adams Armer, 1874–1963

"In the stillness of canyon where only a sheepbell tinkled, or yellow beetles buzzed in the cottonwood trees, the austerity of the land challenged me to produce." (*In Navajo Land,* 1962)

Artist and photographer Laura Adams Armer first travelled to the Navajo Reservation in 1923. "I went first as a painter, trying to express the inner longing for the intangible in a land that is cruel and impersonal. As the years passed, I found myself studying folklore and the religious ritual of sand painting. . . . Only through the kindness extended by various white traders was I enabled to work." (*In Navajo Land,* 1962)

Between 1923 and 1932, Armer witnessed many Navajo ceremonies and formed close friendships with several Navajo singers who "let the white woman come because she wears the turquoise." With Roman Hubbell, she made the first film of the Navajo Mountain Chant in 1928. (*In Navajo Land,* 1962)

Laura Armer spent 40 years interpreting Navajo life to juvenile readers because she recognized "our need to give children something to dream about." (Newberry Medal acceptance speech, 1932)

EDUCATION: Attended public school until age 16, then had private tutor; studied drawing and painting, California School of Design, 1893–99.

FELLOWSHIPS AND AWARDS: Newberry Medal, 1932; Caldecott Medal, 1939.

RESEARCH: Annual ethnographic and painting trips, Navajo and Hopi reservations, 1924–32.

PROFESSIONAL ACTIVITIES: Professional photographer, private photography studio, 1899–1923, specializing in portraiture; Professional artist, specializes in watercolors, 1902–1920s; Professional writer, mid-1920s ff., primarily juvenile books and popular articles illustrated by her husband and herself; produced the first film of a Navajo ceremonial, including a sandpainting, "The Mountain Chant" with Roman Hubbell, 1928; copied more than 100 sandpainting designs for Mary Cabot Wheelwright, 1924–42.

Desert Magazine takes pride in presenting to its readers the first in a series of previously unpublished articles by one of America's most distinguished-- and sensitive-- authorities on the culture of the Navajos:

Laura Adams Armer

author of WATERLESS MOUNTAIN, DARK CIRCLE OF BRANCHES, SOUTHWEST, CACTUS, and THE TRADER'S CHILDREN

Based on her 1923-31 experiences in Navajoland

On January 12, 1960, Laura Armer entered her 87th year. She was born in Sacramento, Calif., the youngest of three children. "Nothing turned to gold for father," she recalls, "but we did have food and drink and books." Her early life in San Francisco centered around an education in art—but the beauty around her was "elusive." After six years in art school, she opened a photography studio. "I was successful," she writes. "I photographed celebrities from all over the world—still I was not satisfied with my medium or with what I was trying to express. Then one day I received an inspiration—as if a voice had spoken. 'Don't worry,' I found myself saying out loud, 'when you are an old woman you will write what you fail to paint.' So I began life over."

In 1923 Laura Armer made her first visit to Navajoland (see following page). A decade of dedicated work followed. "Waterless Mountain," written in 1928, was the first great book to come from her experiences in the Four Corners Country. When it was awarded the Newberry Medal, the prophesy was fulfilled.

Mrs. Armer and her artist husband, Sidney, are "spending our last days surrounded by the groves of beautiful redwoods in northern California."

RECENT PHOTO OF LAURA ARMER

TURN PAGE FOR "NAVAJOLAND IN 1923" ▶

13

Desert Magazine, Vol. 23, No. 3, 1960.

Armer was a prolific author and wrote many accounts of her life on the Navajo reservation for popular journals.

Courtesy of *Desert Magazine*. Photograph by Helga Teiwes. Courtesy of the Arizona State Museum.

Navajo Curing Ceremony, 1905.

As an artist with a keen eye, Armer copied more than 100 Navajo sandpainting designs from the Black Mountain region for Mary Cabot Wheelwright. Trader Roman Hubbell helped her obtain entrance to many ceremonies and introduced her to Nai Nai, a Mountainway singer.

Photograph by Simeon Schwemberger. Courtesy of the Arizona State Museum.

Erna Fergusson, ca. 1932.

In a departure from the usual male cowboys employed by most western resorts, Fergusson used as guides "young women of education and some social grace. . . . They are expected to learn many facts about this country and to impart them in a way of interest to intelligent travelers." (Quoted in Thomas, *The Southwestern Indian Detours,* 1978)

Courtesy of the Museum of New Mexico.

Erna Fergusson, 1888–1964

"The problem is to reconcile 'the ways of the ancients' . . . with the concepts and needs of today." (*New Mexico: A Pageant of Three Peoples,* 1951)

Erna Fergusson was born and raised in New Mexico. After teaching in the Albuquerque public schools, Fergusson began taking tourists to see Indian dances. In the early 1920s, she and Ethel Hickey organized "Koshare Tours." The company was so successful that the Fred Harvey Company purchased it and hired Fergusson to train girl guides for their "Indian Detours."

Fergusson's book about Indian ceremonials, *Dancing Gods* (1931), was the first of many travel books and articles that made the Southwest seem like "real and accessible places for the general reader." A desire to keep progress and profit in balance with the Southwest's geographical and cultural heritage informed her writings which earned her the title of New Mexico's First Lady of Letters.

EDUCATION: B.A., education, University of New Mexico, 1912; M.A., history, Columbia University, 1913.

FELLOWSHIPS AND AWARDS: LL. D., University of New Mexico, 1943.

RESEARCH: Extensive travel in New Mexico 1916–30; Guatemala, Venezuela, Hawaii, Chile, Cuba, Mexico, 1937–46.

PROFESSIONAL ACTIVITIES: Teacher, Chatham Hall, Virginia and Albuquerque, New Mexico, 1913–16; Home Service Supervisor, American Red Cross, 1916–18; Journalist, *The Albuquerque Herald,* 1918–26; Freelance writer, 1926–64; operated Tourist Bureau, Koshare Tours, 1921–26; Chief Courier, Indian Detours, Fred Harvey Company, 1926–51; teaches summer school, University of New Mexico, University of Nebraska, Claremeont College; Speaker in Mexico, Guatemala, South America, Committee on Cultural Relations with Latin America, 1936–56; writes travelogues, guide books and cookbooks; Member, Society of Women Geographers.

Koshare Tours Stop at Tesuque Pueblo, ca. 1935.
Canuto Suazo on right.

Tourists would stop at Pueblos to view architecture and dances and to buy pottery. Fergusson wanted her guests to get 'close' to the land and its inhabitants.

Photograph by T. Harmon Parkhurst. Courtesy of the Museum of New Mexico.

(*top*) Harvey Company Detours Pamphlet with Map of the Rio Grande Pueblos, 1928.

The Harvey Company Indian Detours, like its hotels and Indian arts salerooms, were a "partnership between commercialism and romanticism." (Thomas, *The Southwestern Indian Detours,* 1978)

Courtesy of the Arizona Historical Society.

(*bottom*) Indian Detours Limousine, ca. 1930.

"It is the purpose of the Indian Detour to take you through the very heart of all this, to make you feel the lure of the Southwest." (Detours brochure, 1926)

Courtesy of the Museum of New Mexico.

Mary Colter traveling with construction men by cableway to Indian Gardens at the Grand Canyon in 1923. Colter was a perfectionist and very demanding of her "boys" who referred to her as "Old Lady Colter."

From Virginia Grattan. *Mary Colter: Builder Upon the Red Earth,* 1980. Courtesy of Northland Press.

Mary Elizabeth Jane Colter, 1869–1958

"The primitive architect never intentionally copied anything but made every building suit its own conditions and each one differed from every other according to the character of the *site,* the *materials* that could be procured and the *purpose* for which the building was intended." (*Manual for Drivers and Guides Descriptive of the Indian Watchtower,* 1933)

In addition to her artistic talent, Mary Colter had a strong and determined personality. When her father died suddenly in 1886 leaving a widow and two daughters without financial support, Colter persuaded her mother to send her to art school so that she would be able to support them by teaching art. At age seventeen she began her studies at the California School of Design and worked part-time as an apprentice in a San Francisco architect's office during the years the revival of Spanish architecture in California was beginning.

While teaching mechanical drawing at a St. Paul, Minnesota high school, Colter was offered a temporary job in 1902 with the Fred Harvey Company. The Indian Building adjoining the new Alvarado Hotel in Albuquerque "needed a decorator who knew Indian things and had imagination." In 1905, she was again hired to design a building to house the main salesrooms for Fred Harvey Indian Arts at the Grand Canyon. The result was Hopi House. Colter became a full-time architect and designer for the Fred Harvey Company and the Santa Fe Railroad in 1910. In the next thirty-eight years she created twenty architectural and interior design projects re-creating the Spanish and Indian heritage of the Southwest—structures that were and are critical in introducing the traveling American public to the richness and beauty of Native American art.

EDUCATION: B.A., California School of Design, 1890; takes courses in archaeology, University of Minnesota, ca. 1895; architectural apprentice, San Francisco, 1887–1890

RESEARCH: Studies Pueblo and Navajo arts, design, and architecture, 1902ff.

PROFESSIONAL ACTIVITIES: School teacher, Menonimi, Minnesota, 1890–91; Teacher, Mechanic Arts High School, St. Paul, Minnesota, 1892–1907; Literary Editor, *St. Paul Globe,* late 1890s; Architect, designer, and interior decorator, Fred Harvey Company, 1902–09 (part-time), 1910–41 (full-time); lectures on world history and architecture, University of Minnesota and Century Club in Minnesota and Iowa, 1892–1907; Decorator, Frederick and Nelson Department Store, Seattle, Washington, 1908–10.

Hopi House, Grand Canyon, 1905.

Colter's second project for the Fred Harvey Company was to design a structure to house the Indian arts showroom at the Grand Canyon. Modeled after dwellings at Oraibi, Hopi House combined romanticism, scholarship and commercialism. Hopi artisans lived on the second floor and demonstrated silversmithing, basketry, and pottery-making in the courtyard.

Courtesy of Special Collections, University of Arizona.

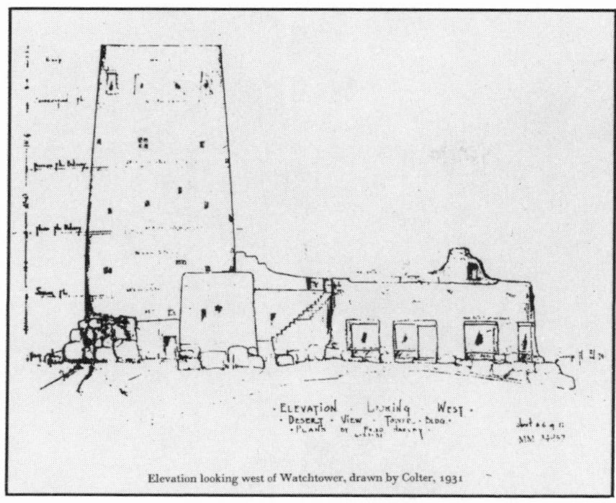
Elevation looking west of Watchtower, drawn by Colter, 1931

Elevation looking west of Watchtower, drawn by Colter, 1931.

When the Fred Harvey Company wanted a rest station-gift shop near the east entrance of the Grand Canyon, Colter decided on an observation tower that would be in harmony with the setting. The Watchtower is a reconstruction of an Anasazi tower. So detailed was the building in its decoration that Colter wrote a 100 page booklet, "Manual for Drivers and Guides Descriptive of the Indian Watchtowers."

From Virginia Grattan. *Mary Colter: Builder Upon the Red Earth,* 1980. Courtesy of Northland Press and Santa Fe Southern Pacific Corporation.

Fred Kabotie painting the Snake legend in the Hopi Room in the Watchtower, 1932.

Colter hired Fred Kabotie, a young Hopi painter and courier to decorate the Hopi Room. Kabotie painted wall frescos based on kiva murals. "Miss Colter was a very talented decorator with strong opinions, and quite elderly. I admired her work, and we got along well . . . most of the time." (*Fred Kabotie: Hopi Indian Artist,* 1977).

From Virginia Grattan. *Mary Colter: Builder Upon the Red Earth,* 1980. Courtesy of Northland Press.

Alice Marriott, 1939.

"It's rather a jolt to find oneself a museum specimen, after a lifetime of display work." (Letter to Nancy Parezo, January, 1986)

Courtesy of Alice Marriott.

Alice Marriott, 1910–

"Like Georgia O'Keeffe, I can say, 'I am not interesting. It is what I have done with where I have been that is'." (Letter to Nancy Parezo and Barbara Babcock, December, 1985)

After receiving the first B.A. in anthropology given to a woman at the University of Oklahoma, Alice Marriott became a field specialist for the Indian Arts and Crafts Board in 1935. In addition to collecting Native American art across the country, she listened to artists' stories and legends. The consequence was *The Ten Grandmothers* (1945), a Kiowa oral history, and the realization that Indian women in particular claimed her attention. The most famous of the Indian women she worked with and wrote about was Maria Martinez, a potter of San Ildefonso Pueblo.

Marriott has worked to make ethnographic reports human stories, writing "for those who did not yet know much about [Indians]." Believing that anthropology is "more than a science, it is a point of view to be shared with as many as possible," she has also written of her personal experiences doing fieldwork. (Quoted in Turner S. Kobler, "Alice Marriott," 1969)

EDUCATION: B.A., English and French, Oklahoma City University, 1930; B.A., anthropology, University of Oklahoma, 1935.
FELLOWSHIPS AND AWARDS: Rockefeller Foundation Grant, 1945–46; Guggenheim Fellowship, 1947, 1948; Bollingen Foundation Grant, 1955, 1956; Neosho Research Award, 1950; University of Oklahoma Achievement Award, 1952; Oklahoma Hall of Fame, 1958; Oklahoma Literary Hall of Fame, 1972.
RESEARCH: Kiowa, 1935–36; Hopi, 1955; throughout Southwest, 1930s–50s; Plains groups, 1935–65.
PROFESSIONAL ACTIVITIES: Librarian, Muskogee Public Library, 1930– 32; Assistant, University of Oklahoma, 1934–36; Field Representative, Indian Arts and Crafts Board, 1936–42; American Red Cross in Texas and New Mexico, 1942–45; Freelance researcher and writer, 1945–85; Governor of Oklahoma's Advisory Committee on the Status of Women, 1948; Associate Director, Southwest Research Associates, 1960–86; Associate Professor, University of Oklahoma, 1964–66; Artist in Residence, Central State University, 1968–70.

Maria and Julian Martinez painting pottery on patio of the Palace of Governors, Santa Fe, New Mexico, 1912.

"Maria Martinez is a woman who has become in her own lifetime a legend. . . . Her strength of character and her skill as a craftswoman are immediately apparent. . . . I, like many other Anglos, have come to regard Mrs. Martinez as a friend." (*Maria, the Potter of San Ildefonso,* 1948)

Photograph by Jesse L. Nusbaum. Courtesy of the Museum of New Mexico.

"Ceremonial meal bowl" made by Maria and Julian Martinez, San Ildefonso Pueblo, 1929. Arizona State Museum, Cat. No. 77-63-3.

This unusual terraced rectangular black-on-black dish was commissioned by Ansel and Virginia Adams as part of a table setting for use in their home. Maria constructed the pot and Julian painted it with a feather motif adapted from a Mimbres pottery design.

Photograph by Helga Teiwes. Courtesy of the Arizona State Museum.

Epilogue

The Gate, Laguna, New Mexico, 1926.

In words that speak for all of us women who have lived and worked with southwestern Native Americans, Mary Austin once remarked that "for those who have been admitted, ever so slightly, to the reality of Indian life, there is a profound and humble thankfulness." (*Taos Pueblo,* 1930)

Photograph by Laura Gilpin. © 1981. Courtesy Laura Gilpin Collection, Amon Carter Museum.

References Cited

BOAS, FRANZ

1928 Keresan Texts. *Publications of the American Ethnological Society,* No. 8.

BROWNE, TURNER AND ELAINE PARTNOW

1983 *Macmillan Biographical Encyclopedia of Photographic Artists and Innovators.* New York: Macmillan.

CHEVIGNY, BELL GALE

1983 Daughters Writing: Toward a Theory of Women's Biography. *Feminist Studies* 9(1):79–102.

COLTON, HAROLD S.

1961 Reminiscences in Southwest Archaeology: IV. *The Kiva* 26(3):1–7.

DENSMORE, FRANCES

1910 Chippewa Music. *Bureau of American Ethnology Bulletin* 45.

1942 The Study of Indian Music. *Smithsonian Annual Report for 1941, Publication 3651.* Pp. 527–550.

DENVER MUSEUM OF NATURAL HISTORY

1985 *Ruth Murray Underhill: Friend of the Desert People.* (Videotape)

DUNN, DOROTHY

1952 Pablita Velarde, Painter of Pueblo Life. *El Palacio* 59(11):338.

FINK, AUGUSTA

1983 *I—Mary, A Biography of Mary Austin.* Tucson: The University of Arizona Press.

GOLDBERG, VICKI

1986 An Eye for Ageless Beauty. *The New York Times Magazine,* January 19:34–37.

GRATTAN, VIRGINIA L.

1980 *Mary Colter: Builder Upon the Red Earth.* Flagstaff, Arizona: Northland Press.

GRIDLEY, MARION E., ED.

1971 *Indians of Today,* 4th edition. ICFP, Inc. Pp. 22–27.

HARE, PETER H.

1985 *A Woman's Quest for Science: Portrait of Anthropologist Elsie Clews Parsons.* Buffalo, New York: Prometheus Books.

HAURY, EMIL W.

1976 *The Hohokam, Desert Farmers and Craftsmen: Excavations at Snaketown, 1964–1965.* Tucson, Arizona: The University of Arizona Press.

HOFFMAN, CHARLES

1946 Frances Densmore and the Music of the American Indian. *Journal of American Folklore* 59(231):45–50.

1968 *Frances Densmore and the American Indian Music.* New York: Museum of the American Indian, Heye Foundation.

HOLMES, WILLIAM H.

1878 Report on the Ancient Ruins of Southwestern Colorado, Examined during the Summers of 1875 and 1876. In *10th Annual Report of the U.S. Geological Survey of the Territories for 1876.* Washington, D.C.: Government Printing Office. Pp. 383–408.

KABOTIE, FRED (WITH BILL BELKNAP)

1977 *Fred Kabotie: Hopi Indian Artist.* Flagstaff, Arizona: Museum of Northern Arizona and Northland Press.

KAMUF, PEGGY

1982 Penelope at Work: Interruptions in *A Room of One's Own. Novel* 16(1):5–18.

KOBLER, TURNER S.

1969 Alice Marriott. *Southwest Writers Series* 27. Austin, Texas: Steck-Vaughn Company.

LANDER, DAWN

1977 Eve Among the Indians. In *The Authority of Experience: Essays in Feminist Criticism,* Arlyn Diamond and Lee R. Edwards, eds. Amherst, Massachusetts: University of Massachusetts Press. Pp. 194–211.

LANGE, CHARLES

1959 *Cochiti: A New Mexico Pueblo, Past and Present.* Austin, Texas: University of Texas Press.

LETSON, NEIL

1984 A Woman of Some Importance. *Connoisseur,* June, 1984: 110–115.

MACKINNON, CATHARINE A.

1982 Feminism, Marxism, Method, and the State: An Agenda for Theory. *Signs* 7(3):515–44.

MEAD, MARGARET

1959 Apprenticeship Under Boas. In *The Anthropology of Franz Boas: Essays on the Centennial of his Birth,* Walter Goldschmidt, ed. *American Anthropological Association Memoir* No. 89.

PANDEY, TRILOKI NATH

1972 Anthropologists at Zuni. *Proceedings of the American Philosophical Society* 116(4):321–337.

PARSONS, ELSIE CLEWS

1913 *The Old-Fashioned Woman: Primitive Fancies About the Sex.* New York: G.P. Putnam's Sons.

1916 *Social Rule: A Study of the Will to Power.* New York: G.P. Putnam's Sons.

PITTS, TERANCE R.

1981 The Early Work of Laura Gilpin, 1917–1932. *Center for Creative Photogrpahy, University of Arizona Research Series* Number 13. Pp. 7–9.

SPIER, LESLIE R. AND A. L. KROEBER

1943 Elsie Clews Parsons. *American Anthropologist* 45(2): 244–255.

STEVENSON, JAMES

1883 Illustrated Catalog of the Collections Obtained from the Indians of New Mexico and Arizona in 1879 and 1880. *2nd Annual Report, Bureau of American Ethnology.* Pp. 307–422.

STEWART, IRENE

1980 *A Voice in Her Tribe.* Socorro, New Mexico: Ballena Press.

THOMAS, D. H.

1978 *The Southwestern Indian Detours.* Phoenix, Arizona: Hunter Publishing Company.

VESTAL, DAVID

1977 Laura Gilpin: Photographer of the Southwest. *Popular Photography* 80: 100–101, 130–134.

WYMAN, LELAND C. AND HARRISON BEGAY

1967 *The Sacred Mountain of the Navajo.* Flagstaff: Museum of Northern Arizona.

ZWINGER, ANN

1987 Writers of the Purple Figwort. In *Old Southwest, New Southwest,* Judy Nolte Lensink, ed. Tucson, Arizona: The Tucson Public Library. Pp. 143–154.

Selected Southwest Bibliography

AITKEN, BARBARA FREIRE-MARRECO

1914 Tewa Kinship Terms from the Pueblo of Hano, Arizona. *American Anthropologist* 16(2):269–287.

1916 *Ethnobotany of the Tewa Indians.* (with Wilfred W. Robbins and John P. Harrington) *Bureau of American Ethnology Bulletin* No. 55.

1923 Conception. *El Palacio* 14(6):79–81.

1924 A Tewa Craftsman: Leslie Agayo. *El Palacio* 17(5):91–97.

1927 The Morning Star of the Southwest. *American Anthropologist* 29(4):731–732.

1930 Temperament in Native American Religion. *Journal of the Royal Anthropological Institute* 60:363–387.

1931 Folk-history and Its Raw Material: White Men's Raids on the Hopi Villages. *New Mexico Historical Review* 6(4):376–382.

1949 A Note on Pueblo Belt-Weaving. *Man* 49(46):37.

ARMER, LAURA ADAMS

1925 A Navaho Sand Painting. *University of California Chronicle* 27:233–239.

1928 *Waterless Mountain.* New York: Longmans, Green.

1929 Navajo Sand Painters at Their Work. *Travel* 53(Aug.)

1931 Navajo Sandpaintings. *American Anthropologist* 33:657.

1931 Sand-Painting of the Navaho Indians. *Introduction to American Indian Art.* Part II, Leaflet No. 5. New York: Exposition of Indian Tribal Arts.

1933 *Dark Circle of Branches.* New York: Longmans, Green.

1935 *Southwest.* New York: Longmans, Green.

1937 *The Trader's Children.* New York: Longmans, Green.

1950 Two Navaho Sand-Paintings with Certain Comparisons. *The Masterkey* 24(2):79–83.

1953 The Crawler, Navaho Healer. *The Masterkey* 27(1):5–10.

1962 *In Navajo Land.* New York: David McKay.

AUSTIN, MARY

1903 *The Land of Little Rain.* Boston, Massachusetts: Houghton Mifflin.

1904 *The Basket Woman.* Boston, Massachusetts: Houghton Mifflin.

1909 *Lost Borders.* New York: Harper.

1911 *The Arrow Maker.* New York: Duffield.

1914 *California, Land of the Sun.* London: Black.

1923 *The American Rhythm.* New York: Harcourt Brace.

1924 *The Land of Journey's Ending.* New York: Century.

1924 The Days of Our Ancients. *Survey* 53:33–38,59.

1928 *The Children Sing in the Far West.* Boston, Massachusetts: Houghton Mifflin.

1928 Indian Arts for Indians. *Survey Graphics* 13(4):381–388.

1930 *Taos Pueblo.* (with photographs by Ansel Adams) San Francisco, California: Grabhorn.

1931 Indian Poetry. *Introduction to American Indian Art.* Part II. Leaflet No. 3. New York: Exposition of Indian Tribal Arts.

1931 *Starry Adventure.* New York: Houghton Mifflin.

1932 *Earth Horizon: An Autobiography.* Boston, Massachusetts: Houghton Mifflin.

1933 Folk Plays of the Southwest. *Theatre Arts* 17:599–610.

1933 American Indian Murals. *Magazine of Art* 26(8):380–384.

1934 *Indian Pottery of the Rio Grande.* Pasadena, California: Esto.

BARTLETT, KATHARINE

1930 Stone Artifacts: San Francisco Mountain Region. *Museum Notes* 3(6):1–4.

1931 Prehistoric Pueblo Foods. *Museum Notes* 4(4):1–4.

1932 A Unique Pueblo II Bird Fetish. *American Anthropologist* 34:315–319.

1933 The Indians of Northern Arizona. *Museum Notes* 5(12):65–70.

1933 Pueblo Milling Stones of the Flagstaff Region and Their Relation to Others in the Southwest. *Museum of Northern Arizona Bulletin* No. 3.

1934 Spanish Contacts with the Hopi, 1540–1823. *Museum Notes* 6(12):55–60.

1936 The Utilization of Maize Among the Ancient Pueblos. In Symposium on Prehistoric Agriculture. *University of New Mexico Bulletin,* Anthropological Series 1(5):29–34.

1936 How to Appreciate Hopi Handicrafts. *Museum Notes* 9(1):1–8.

1942 Notes Upon the Routes of Espejo and Farfan to the Mines in the 16th Century. *New Mexico Historical Review* 17(1):21–36.

1945 The Distribution of the Indians of Arizona in 1848. *Plateau* 17(3):41–45.

1949 Hopi Yucca Baskets. *Plateau* 21(3):33–41.

1949 Hopi Indian Costume. *Plateau* 22(1):1–10.

1953 25 Years of Anthropology. *Plateau* 26(1):38–60.

1977 A History of Hopi Pottery. *Plateau* 49(3):2–13.

BENEDICT, RUTH

1929 The Science of Custom. *Century Magazine* 117:641–9.

1930 Psychological Types in the Cultures of the Southwest. *Proceedings, 23rd International Congress of Americanists:* 572–81. New York.

1930 Eight Stories from Acoma. *Journal of American Folklore* 43(167):59–87.

1931 Tales of the Cochiti Indians. *Bureau of American Ethnology Bulletin* No. 98.

1932 Configurations of Cultures in North America. *American Anthropologist* 34(1):1–27.

1934 *Patterns of Culture.* Boston, Massachusetts: Houghton Mifflin.

1935 Zuni Mythology. 2 volumes. *Columbia University Contributions to Anthropology* No. 21.

1943 Two Patterns of Indian Acculturation. *American Anthropologist* 45:207–12.

1959 *An Anthropologist at Work: The Writings of Ruth Benedict,* ed. Margaret Mead. Boston, Massachusetts: Houghton Mifflin Company.

BUNZEL, RUTH

1928 Notes on the Kachina Cult in San Felipe. *Journal of American Folklore* 41(160):290–292.

1928 The Emergence. *Journal of American Folklore* 41(160):288–290.

1929 The Pueblo Potter: A Study of Creative Imagination in Primitive Art. *Columbia University Contributions to Anthropology* No. 8.

1929 Psychology of the Pueblo Potter. In *Primitive Heritage,* ed. Margaret Mead and Nicolas Calas. New York: Random House, 266–275.

1932 Introduction to Zuni Ceremonialism. *47th Annual Report of the Bureau of American Ethnology for 1929–1930:* 467–544.

1932 Zuni Origin Myths. *47th Annual Report of the Bureau of American Ethnology for 1929–1930:* 545–609.

1932 Zuni Ritual Poetry. *47th Annual Report of the Bureau of American Ethnology for 1929–1930:* 611–835.

1932 Zuni Kachinas: An Analytical Study. *47th Annual Report of the Bureau of American Ethnology for 1929–1930:* 837–1086.

1933 *Zuni Texts.* New York: G.E. Stechert.

1935 Zuni. In *Handbook of American Indian Languages,* ed. Franz Boas, Vol.3:389–415. New York: J.J. Augustin.

1938 Zuni. *Bureau of American Ethnology Bulletin* 40(3):389–415.

1952 Chichicastenango. A Guatemalan Village. *Publications of the American Ethnological Society* No. 22.

1955 Gladys A. Reichard: A Tribute. Memorial Service, Barnard College, New York.

BURLIN, NATALIE CURTIS

1903 An American-Indian Composer. *Harper's Monthly Magazine* 107(1140):626–632.

1904 The Shepherd Poet: A Bit of Arizona Life. *The Southern Workman* 33(3):145–148.

1904 An Indian Song on a Desert Path. *The Southern Workman* 33(6):344–345.

1904 The Value of Indian Art. *The Southern Workman* 33(8):448–450.

1904 A Bit of American Folk-Music: Two Pueblo Indian Grinding Songs. *Craftsman* 7(1):35–41.

1905 *Songs of Ancient America.* New York: G. Schirmer.

1907 *The Indians' Book.* New York: Harper & Bros.

1908 The Song of the Indian Mother. *Craftsman* 15(1):57–63.

1913 The Perpetuating of Indian Art. *The Outlook* 105:623–631.

1915 Folk Song and the American Indian. *The Southern Workman* 44(9):476–480.
1918 The Indians' Part in the Dedication of the New Museum. *Art and Archaeology* 7(1–2):31–32.
1919 Mr. Roosevelt and Indian Music. *The Outlook* 121(10):399–400.
1919 Theodore Roosevelt in Hopi-Land. *The Outlook* 123(8):87–88, 92–93.
1919 Our Native Craftsmen. *El Palacio* 7(3):51–53.
1920 An American Indian Artist. *The Outlook* 124(1):64–66.
1920 A Plea for our Native Art. *The Musical Quarterly* 6(2):175–178.
1921 American Indian Cradle Songs. *The Musical Quarterly* 7(4):549–58.
1922 Pueblo Poetry. *The Freeman*, January 25, 1922. Reprinted in *El Palacio* 12(7):95–99.

COLLIER, MALCOLM
1939 Navajo Clans and Marriage at Pueblo Alto. (with Katherine Spencer and Doriane Woolley) *American Anthropologist* 41(2):245–257.
1946 Leadership at Navajo Mountain and Klagetoh. *American Anthropologist* 48(1):137–138.
1966 *Local Organization among the Navaho.* HRAFLEX Books, Human Relations Area Files. New Haven, Connecticut.

COLTER, MARY ELIZABETH
1902 Alvarado Hotel and Indian Building, Albuquerque, New Mexico.
1905 Hopi House and El Tovar, Grand Canyon, Arizona.
1910 El Ortiz Hotel, Lamy, New Mexico.
1914–22 Lookout, Hermit's Rest, Phantom Ranch, Grand Canyon, Arizona.
1925 La Fonda Hotel, Santa Fe, New Mexico.
1930 La Posada Hotel, Winslow, Arizona.
1932–35 Watchtower, Bright Angel Lodge, Grand Canyon, Arizona.
1933 *Manual for Drivers and Guides Descriptive of the Indian Watchtower at Desert View and Its Relation, Architecturally, to the Prehistoric Ruins of the Southwest.* Grand Canyon, Arizona: Fred Harvey.

COLTON, MARY-RUSSELL F.
1918 The Little-known Small House Ruins in the Coconino Forest. (with Harold S. Colton) *Memoirs of the American Anthropological Association* 5(4):101–126.
1930 The Hopi Craftsman. *Museum Notes* 3(1):1–4.
1931 Technique of Major Hopi Crafts. *Museum Notes* 3(12):1–7.
1931 Petroglyphs, the Record of a Great Adventure. (with Harold S. Colton) *American Anthropologist* 33(1):32–37.
1932 Hopi Legends of the Sunset Crater Region. (with Edmund Nequatewa) *Museum Notes* 5(4):17–23.
1933 Hopi Courtship and Marriage, Second Mesa. (with Edmund Nequatewa) *Museum Notes* 5(9):41–54.
1934 Art for the Schools of the Southwest. An Outline for the Public and Indian Schools. *Museum of Northern Arizona Bulletin* No. 6.
1938 The Arts and Crafts of the Hopi Indians. *Museum Notes* 11(1):1–24.
1939 Hopi Silversmithing—Its Background and Future. *Plateau* 12(1):1–7.
1965 *Hopi Dyes.* Flagstaff, Arizona: Northland Press.

DENSMORE, FRANCES
1909 Scale Formation in Primitive Music. *American Anthropologist* 11(1):1–2.
1926 American Indian Poetry. *American Anthropologist* 28(4):447–449.
1929 Papago Music. *Bureau of American Ethnology Bulletin* No. 90.
1932 Resemblance between Yuman and Pueblo Songs. *American Anthropologist* 34:694–700.
1936 *The American Indians and Their Music.* New York: The Woman's Press.
1938 Music of Santo Domingo Pueblo, New Mexico. *Southwest Museum Papers* No. 12.
1953 Technique in the Music of the American Indians. *Bureau of American Ethnology Bulletin* No. 151.
1957 Music of Acoma, Isleta, Cochiti, and Zuni Pueblos. *Bureau of American Ethnology Bulletin* No. 165.

DUTTON, BERTHA P.
1936 The Laguna Calendar. (with Miriam A. Marmon) *University of New Mexico Bulletin* 238, Anthropological Series 1(2).
1938 Leyit Kin, a Small House Ruin in Chaco Canyon, New Mexico. *School of American Research Monograph* No. 1(5).
1941 The Navajo Wind Way Ceremonial. *El Palacio* 48(4):73–82.
1943 A History of Plumbate Ware. *Papers of the School of American Research* No. 50.

1947 Girl Scout Archaeological Expedition. *El Palacio* 54:191–94.

1948 *New Mexico Indians.* Santa Fe, New Mexico: Museum of New Mexico.

1957 Indian Artistry in Wood and Other Media. *El Palacio* 64:3–28.

1961 Navajo Weaving Today. *Museum of New Mexico, Popular Series Handbook* No. 2.

1962 *Let's Explore! Indian Villages Past and Present.* Santa Fe, New Mexico: Museum of New Mexico Press.

1962 *Happy People: The Huichol Indians.* Santa Fe, New Mexico: Museum of New Mexico Press.

1962 *Sun Father's Way: The Kiva Murals of Kuaua.* Albuquerque, New Mexico: University of New Mexico Press.

1964 Mesoamerican Culture Traits Which Appear in the American Southwest. *Proceedings of the 35th International Congress of Americanists* 1:481–492.

1975 *Indians of the American Southwest.* Englewood Cliffs, New Jersey: Prentice-Hall.

1978 *Myths and Legends of the Indians of the Southwest.* (with Caroline B. Olin) San Francisco, California: Bellerophon Books.

ELLIS, FLORENCE HAWLEY

1929 Prehistoric Pottery Pigments in the Southwest. *American Anthropologist* 31(4):731–754.

1934 The Significance of the Dated Prehistory of Chetro Ketl, Chaco Canyon, New Mexico. *University of New Mexico Bulletin, Monograph Series* 1, No. 1.

1936 Field Manual of Prehistoric Southwestern Pottery Types. *University of New Mexico Bulletin* 238, Anthropological Series 1(1).

1936 *Tseh So: A Small House Ruin, Chaco Canyon, New Mexico.* (with D.D. Brand and F.C. Hibben) Albuquerque, New Mexico: University of New Mexico Press.

1937 Pueblo Social Organization as a Lead to Pueblo History. *American Anthropologist* 39(3):504–526.

1946 The Role of Pueblo Social Organization in the Dissemination of Catholicism. *American Anthropologist* 48(3):407–415.

1950 Big Kivas, Little Kivas and Moiety Houses in Historical Reconstruction. *Southwestern Journal of Anthropology* 6:286–.302.

1959 Archaeological and Ethnological Data Pertaining to Acoma and Laguna Land Claims, 1958–1959. Manuscript in New Mexico Archaeological Center, University of New Mexico.

1964 *A Reconstruction of the Basic Jemez Pattern of Social Organization.* Albuquerque, New Mexico: University of New Mexico Press.

1966 The Immediate History of Zia Pueblo as Derived from Excavation in Refuse Deposits. *American Antiquity* 31:806–811.

1974 Anthropological Data Pertaining to the Taos Land Claim. *American Indian Ethnohistory. Pueblo Indians* 1. New York: Garland.

1979 Isleta Pueblo. In *Handbook of North American Indians.* Southwest, Vol. 9. Washington, D.C.: Smithsonian Institution Press, 351–365.

FERGUSSON, ERNA

1923 Acoma, the City of the Sky. *New Mexico Highway Journal* 1:4–5.

1931 Ceremonial Dances of the Pueblo. *Travel* 58(12):15–19.

1931 *Dancing Gods: Indian Ceremonials of New Mexico and Arizona.* New York: Alfred A. Knopf.

1933 Laughing Priests. *Theatre Arts* 17(8):657–662.

1934 Indians of Mexico and New Mexico. *New Mexico Quarterly* 4(3):169–73.

1940 *Our Southwest.* New York: Alfred A. Knopf.

1951 *New Mexico, A Pageant of Three Peoples.* New York: Alfred A. Knopf.

1951 Modern Apaches of New Mexico. *The American Indian* 6(3):3–14.

GILLMOR, FRANCES

1930 *Windsinger.* New York: Minton, Balch, and Co.

1934 *Traders to the Navajos: The Story of the Wetherills of Kayenta* (with Louisa Wade Wetherill). Boston, Massachusetts: Houghton, Mifflin and Co.

1943 The Dance Dramas of Mexican Villages. *University of Arizona Humanities Bulletin* No. 5.

1945 Opportunities in Arizona Folklore. *University of Arizona Bulletin* Vol. XVI. General Bulletin No. 9.

1945 The Wetherills of Kayenta. *The Kiva* 11(1):9–11.

1949 *Flute of the Smoking Mirror.* Albuquerque, New Mexico: University of New Mexico Press.

1978 *The King Danced in the Marketplace.* Salt Lake City, Utah: University of Utah Press.

GILPIN, LAURA

1926 Dream Pictures of My People. *Art and Archaeology* 22:12–20.

1927 *The Mesa Verde National Park: Reproductions from a Series of Photographs.* Colorado Springs, Colorado: The Gilpin Co.

1940 *New Mexico: A Guide to the Colorful State.* WPA Guide Series. New York: Hastings House.

1941 *The Pueblos: A Camera Chronicle.* New York: Hastings House.

1949 *The Rio Grande, River of Destiny: An Interpretation of the River, the Land, and the People.* New York: Duell, Sloan, and Pearce.

1968 *The Enduring Navaho.* Austin, Texas: University of Texas Press.

1971 In Memoriam: Popovi Da of San Ildefonso. *El Palacio* 78(1):45.

1973 *A Taos Mosaic.* Albuquerque, New Mexico: Claire Morrill.

GOLDFRANK, ESTHER S.

1921 A Note on Twins. *American Anthropologist* 23:387–388.

1923 Notes on Two Pueblo Feasts. *American Anthropologist* 25(2):188–196.

1926 Isleta Variants: A Study in Flexibility. *Journal of American Folklore* 39(15):70–78.

1927 The Social and Ceremonial Organization of Cochiti. *Memoirs of the American Anthropological Association* No. 33.

1943 Some Aspects of Pueblo Mythology and Society. (with Karl A. Wittfogel) *Journal of American Folklore* 56(219):17–30.

1945 Irrigation Agriculture and Navajo Community Leadership: Case Material on Environment and Culture. *American Anthropologist* 47(2):262–277.

1945 Socialization, Personality, and the Structure of Pueblo Society. *American Anthropologist* 47(4):516–540.

1946 More about Irrigation Agriculture and Navajo Community Leadership. *American Anthropologist* 48(3):473–82.

1946 Linguistic Note to Zuni Ethnology. *Word* 2(3):191–96.

1948 The Impact of Situation and Personality on Four Hopi Emergence Myths. *Southwest Journal of Anthropology* 4(3):241–262.

1952 The Different Patterns of Blackfoot and Pueblo Adaptation to White Authority. In *Acculturation in the Americas,* ed. Sol Tax. Chicago, Illinois: University of Chicago Press, 74–79.

1954 Notes on Deer-Hunting Practices at Laguna Pueblo, New Mexico. *Texas Journal of Science* 6(4):407–21.

1955 Native Paintings of Isleta Pueblo, New Mexico. *Transactions of the New York Academy of Sciences,* Series II. 18(2):178–80.

1962 Ed. *Isleta Paintings.* (Introduction and Commentary by E. C. Parsons) *Bureau of American Ethnology Bulletin* No. 181.

1967 The Artist of "Isleta Paintings" in Pueblo Society. *Smithsonian Contributions to Anthropology* No. 5.

1978 *Notes on an Undirected Life, as One Anthropologist Tells It.* Flushing, New York: Queens College Press.

1983 Another View: Margaret and Me. *Ethnohistory* 30(1): 1–14.

1985 Two Anthropologists—the Same Informant: Some Differences in the Recorded Data. *Journal of the Anthropological Society of Oxford* 16(1):42–52.

HALPERN, KATHERINE SPENCER

1939 Navajo Clans and Marriage at Pueblo Alto. (with Malcolm Collier and Doriane Woolley) *American Anthropologist* 41(2):245–257.

1940 *A Bibliography of the Navaho Indians.* (with Clyde Kluckhohn) New York: J.J. Augustin.

1947 Reflections of Social Life in the Navaho Origin Myth. *University of New Mexico Publication in Anthropology* No. 3.

1955 *Sociocultural Elements in Casework: A Casebook of Seven Ethnic Case Studies.* New York: Council on Social Work Education.

1957 Mythology and Values: An Analysis of Navaho Chantway Myths. *Memoirs of the American Folklore Society* No. 48.

1960 The Family and Child Development: A Sociocultural Viewpoint. In *The Healthy Child,* ed. H.D. Stuart and D.G. Prugh. Cambridge, Massachusetts: Harvard University Press, 340–48.

1965 Integrating Social Work into a Hospital

Program. (with G. Edinburg) *Mental Hospitals* 16:215–218.

1965 Impoverished Navajo Indians are Stark Culture Contrast. *SSW Views,* Boston University Publication, November 8, 1965.

1971 Navajo Health and Welfare Aides: A Field Study. *The Social Service Review* 45:37–52.

HEGEMANN, ELIZABETH C.

1961 *A Collection of Photographs of the Navajo and Hopi Country, 1922–1932.* Flagstaff, Arizona: Northern Arizona Society of Science and Art.

1963 *Navaho Trading Days.* Albuquerque, New Mexico: University of New Mexico Press.

KELLY, ISABEL T.

1934 Southern Paiute Bands. *American Anthropologist* 36:548–560.

1936 Chemehuevi Shamanism. In *Essays in Anthropology.* Berkeley: University of California Press, 129–142.

1944 West Mexico and the Hohokam. In *El Norte de Mexico y el Sur de Estados Unidos, Tercera Reunion de Mesa Redonda Sobre Problems Antropologicas de Mexico y Centro America.* Mexico, D.F.: Sociedad Mexicana de Anthropologia, 206–222.

1945 Excavations at Culican, Sinaloa. *Ibero-Americana* 25:1–186.

1965 Folk Practices in North Mexico: Birth Customs, Folk Medicine, and Spiritualism in the Laguna Zone. *Latin American Monographs* No. 2. Austin, Texas: University of Texas Press.

1978 The Hodges Ruin: A Hohokam Community in the Tucson Basin. (with James Officer and Emil W. Haury) *University of Arizona Anthropological Papers* No. 30.

KENT, KATE PECK

1940 The Braiding of a Hopi Wedding Sash. *Plateau* 12(3):46–52.

1941 Notes on the Weaving of Prehistoric Pueblo Textiles. *Plateau* 14(1):1–11.

1945 A Comparison of Prehistoric and Modern Pueblo Weaving. *The Kiva* 10(2):14–20.

1954 Textiles. In Montezuma Castle Archaeology, Part 2. *Southwest Monuments Association Technical Series* 3(2):1–102.

1957 The Cultivation and Weaving of Cotton in the Prehistoric Southwestern United States. *Transactions of the American Philosophical Society* 47(3):457–733.

1961 *The Story of Navajo Weaving.* Phoenix, Arizona: The Heard Museum.

1966 Archaeological Clues to Early Historic Navajo and Pueblo Weaving. *Plateau* 39(1):46–60.

1976 Pueblo and Navajo Weaving Traditions and the Western World. In *Ethnic and Tourist Arts: Cultural Expressions from the Fourth World,* ed. Nelson H.H. Graburn. Berkeley, California: University of California Press, 85–101.

1981 Pueblo Weaving. *American Indian Art Magazine* 7(1):32–45.

1983 *Prehistoric Textiles of the Southwest.* Albuquerque, New Mexico: University of New Mexico Press.

1983 *Pueblo Indian Textiles: A Living Tradition.* Santa Fe, New Mexico: School of American Research Press.

1985 *Navajo Weaving.* Santa Fe, New Mexico: School of American Research Press.

KEUR, DOROTHY L.

1941 Big Bead Mesa: An Archaeological Study of Navaho Acculturation, 1745–1812. *Memoirs of the Society for American Archaeology* No. 1.

1944 A Chapter in Navaho-Pueblo Relations. *American Antiquity* 10:75–86.

KURATH, GERTRUDE P.

1953 Native Choreographic Areas of North America. *American Anthropologist* 55(1):153–162.

1957 The Origins of the Pueblo Indian Matachines. *El Palacio* 64(9–10):259–264.

1958 Game Animal Dances of the Rio Grande Pueblo Indians. *Southwestern Journal of Anthropology* 14(4):438–448.

1958 Plaza Circuits of Tewa Indian Dances. *El Palacio* 65(1):16–26.

1959 Cochiti Choreographies and Songs. Appendix to *Cochiti. A New Mexico Pueblo, Past and Present* by Charles Lange. Austin, Texas: University of Texas Press.

1960 Calling the Rain Gods. *Journal of American Folklore* 73(290):312–316.

1963 Tewa Plaza Dances: A Photo Essay. *American Indian Tradition,* 9(1): 16–20.

1965 Tewa Choreographic Music. In *Studies in Ethnomusicology.* Vol. 2, ed. Mieczyshaw Kolinski. New York: Oak.

1966 The Kinetic Ecology of Yaqui Dance Instrumentation. *Ethnomusicology* 10(1): 28–43.

1970 *Music and Dance of the Tewa Pueblos.* (with Antonio Garcia) Santa Fe, New Mexico: Museum of New Mexico Press. Research Record No. 8.

1986 *Half a Century of Dance Research.* Flagstaff, Arizona: Cross-Cultural Dance Resources.

LAMBERT, MARJORIE F.

1935 The Material from Kuaua. *El Palacio* 38(21–23):119–122.

1936 Observations on the Mission Uncovered at Puaray. *El Palacio* 41:63–66.

1937 A Preliminary Account of the Excavations of Paako, San Antonio, New Mexico. *New Mexico Anthropologist* 1(5):73–77.

1938 The Kivas of Paako and Kuaua. *New Mexico Anthropologist* 2(4–5):71–80.

1941 Six Game Pieces from Otowi. *El Palacio* 48(1):1–6.

1946 Pun-Ku, Kiva Ringing Stones. *El Palacio* 53:42–43.

1946 New Mexico's First Capital. *New Mexico Historical Review* 31(2):140–144.

1947 A Painted Ceremonial Room at Otowi. *El Palacio* 54(3):59–69.

1952 Oldest Armor in United States Discovered at San Gabriel del Yunque. *El Palacio* 59:83–87.

1953 The Oldest Armor Found in the United States—the San Gabriel del Yunque Helmet. *Archaeology* 6(2):108–110.

1954 Paa-ko: Archaeological Chronicle of an Indian Village in North-central New Mexico. *School of American Research Monograph* No. 19.

1956 Rare Glaze I-Yellow Potsherd from San Cristobal. *El Palacio* 63(2):35.

1956 Some Clay and Stone Figurines from the Mogollon-Mimbres Area, Luna County, New Mexico. *El Palacio* 63:259–283.

1957 A Rare Stone Humpbacked Figure from Pecos Pueblo, New Mexico. *El Palacio* 64(3–4):103–108.

1958 A Pottery Bell from Northwestern New Mexico. *American Antiquity* 24(2):184–185.

1964 Cave Survey and Excavations in Hidalgo County, New Mexico. (with Richard Ambler) *School of American Research Monograph* No. 24.

1965 *Southwest Indians Today: A Gallery Guide.* Santa Fe, New Mexico: Museum of New Mexico Press.

1966 *Pueblo Indian Pottery: Materials, Tools and Techniques.* Museum of New Mexico, Popular Series, Pamphlet No. 5.

1979 Pojoaque Pueblo. Vol 9. Southwest. *Handbook of North American Indians.* Washington, D.C.: Smithsonian Institution Press, 324–329.

1969 Mural Decorations in the San Jose de los Jemez Mission Church. In *Collected Papers in Honor of Bertha P. Dutton.* Papers of the Archaeological Society of New Mexico No. 4.

1981 Spanish Influences on the Pottery of San Jose de los Jemez and Guisewa. In *Collected Papers in Honor of Erik Reed.* Papers of the Archaeological Society of New Mexico No. 6.

LEIGHTON, DOROTHEA C.

1941 Elements of Psychotherapy in Navaho Religion. (with Alexander Leighton) *Psychiatry* 4(4):515–523.

1942 Some Types of Uneasiness and Fear in a Navaho Indian Community. (with Alexander Leighton) *American Anthropologist* 44(1):194–209.

1944 *The Navaho Door: An Introduction to Navaho Life.* (with Alexander Leighton) Cambridge, Massachusetts: Harvard University Press.

1946 *The Navajo.* (with Clyde Kluckhohn) Cambridge, Massachusetts: Harvard University Press.

1947 *Children of the People: The Navaho Individual and His Development.* (with Clyde Kluckhohn) Cambridge, Massachusetts: Harvard University Press.

1949 Gregorio the Hand-Trembler: A Psychobiological Personality Study of a Navajo Indian. (with Alexander Leighton) *Peabody Museum Papers* 40(1).

1966 *People of the Middle Place: A Study of the Zuni Indians.* (with John Adair) New Haven, Connecticut: Human Relations Area Files Press.

1982 As I Knew Them: Navajo Women in 1940. *American Indian Quarterly* 6(1–2):43–51.

MARRIOT, ALICE LEE

1945 *The Ten Grandmothers.* Norman, Oklahoma: University of Oklahoma Press.

1948 *Maria: The Potter of San Ildefonso.* Norman, Oklahoma: University of Oklahoma Press.

1949 *These Are the People; Some Notes on the Southwestern Indians*. Santa Fe, New Mexico: Laboratory of Anthropology.

1949 *The Valley Below*. Norman, Oklahoma: University of Oklahoma Press.

1952 *Indians of the Four Corners: A Book About the Anasazi Indians and Their Modern Descendants*. New York: Thomas T. Crowell.

1968 *American Indian Mythology*. (with Carol K. Rachlin) New York: Crowell.

1969 *American Epic: The Story of the American Indian*. (with Carol K. Rachlin) New York: Putnam.

NEWCOMB, FRANC JOHNSON

1936 Symbols in Sand. *Indian Art Series* No. 11. Santa Fe, New Mexico: New Mexico Association on Indian Affairs.

1937 *Sandpaintings of the Navaho Shooting Chant*. (with Gladys Reichard) New York: J.J. Augustin.

1938 The Navajo Listening Rite. *El Palacio* 45(9–11):46–49.

1940 *Navaho Omens and Taboos*. Santa Fe, New Mexico: Rydal.

1940 Origin Legend of the Navaho Eagle Chant. *Journal of American Folklore* 50(207):50–77.

1956 A Study of Navajo Symbolism. (with Stanley Fishler and Mary C. Wheelwright) *Papers of the Peabody Museum* 32(3). Cambridge, Massachusetts: Harvard University Press.

1962 Sandpaintings of Beautyway. (with Leland C. Wyman) *Plateau* 35(2):37–52.

1963 Drypaintings Used in Divination by the Navajo. *Plateau* 36(1):18–24.

1964 *Hosteen Klah, Navaho Medicine Man and Sandpainter*. Norman, Oklahoma: University of Oklahoma Press.

1966 *Navaho Neighbors*. Norman, Oklahoma: University of Oklahoma Press.

1967 *Navaho Folk Tales*. (Foreword by Bertha Dutton) Santa Fe, New Mexico: Museum of Navaho Ceremonial Art.

1970 *Navaho Bird Tales*. Wheaton, Illinois: Quest Books.

PAINTER, MURIEL

1950 *The Yaqui Easter Ceremony at Pascua*. Tucson, Arizona: Tucson Chamber of Commerce.

1955 A Yaqui Easter Sermon. (with Refugio Savala and Ignacio Alvarez) *University of Arizona Social Science Bulletin* No. 26.

1960 *Easter at Pascua Village*. Tucson, Arizona: The University of Arizona Press.

1962 *Faith, Flowers and Fiestas*. (with E.B. Sayles) Tucson, Arizona: The University of Arizona Press for the Arizona State Museum.

1970 *A Yaqui Easter*. Tucson, Arizona: The University of Arizona Press.

1980 *The Autobiography of a Yaqui Poet by Refugio Savala*. (Kathleen M. Sands, editor) Tucson, Arizona: The University of Arizona Press.

1986 *With a Good Heart: Yaqui Beliefs and Ceremonies in Pascua Village*. Tucson, Arizona: The University of Arizona Press.

PARSONS, ELSIE CLEWS

n.d. In the Southwest. Unpublished manuscript, American Philosophical Society.

1917 Ceremonial Friendship at Zuni. *American Anthropologist* 19(1):1–8.

1917 Notes on the Zuni, Parts I and II. *Memoirs of the American Anthropological Association* Nos. 19 and 20.

1919 Mothers and Children at Zuni, New Mexico. *Man* 19:168–173.

1920 Notes on Ceremonialism at Laguna. *Anthropological Papers of the American Museum of Natural History* 19(4):85–131.

1922 Contributions to Hopi History: Oraibi in 1920. *American Anthropologist* 24(3):283–298.

1922 Ed. *American Indian Life*. New York: Huebsch.

1923 Laguna Genealogies. *Anthropological Papers of the American Museum of Natural History* 19(5):133–292.

1924 Tewa Kin, Clan and Moiety. *American Anthropologist* 26(3):333–349.

1925 *The Pueblo of Jemez*. New Haven, Connecticut: Yale University Press.

1926 Tewa Tales. *Memoirs of the American Folklore Society* No. 19.

1928 Notes on the Pima, 1926. *American Anthropologist* 30:445–464.

1929 The Social Organization of the Tewa of New Mexico. *Memoirs of the American Anthropological Association* No. 36.

1930 Spanish Elements in the Kachina Cult of the Pueblos. *Proceedings of the International Congress of Americanists for 1928* No. 23:582–603.

1933 Hopi and Zuni Ceremonialism. *Memoirs of the American Anthropological Association* No. 39.

1936 Taos Pueblo. *AAA General Series in Anthropology* No. 2.

1939 *Pueblo Indian Religion.* 2 volumes. Chicago, Illinois: University of Chicago Press.

1940 Relations Between Ethnology and Archaeology in the Southwest. *American Antiquity* 5(3):214–220.

REICHARD, GLADYS A.

1928 Social Life of the Navaho. *Columbia University Contributions to Anthropology* No. 7.

1934 *Spider Woman: A Story of Navaho Weavers and Chanters.* New York: Macmillan.

1936 *Navaho Shepherd and Weaver.* New York: J.J. Augustin.

1937 *Sandpaintings of the Navaho Shooting Chant.* (with Franc J. Newcomb) New York: J.J. Augustin.

1938 Social Life. In *General Anthropology,* ed. Franz Boas. New York: D.C. Heath, 409–86.

1939 *Dezba: Woman of the Desert.* New York: J.J. Augustin.

1939 *Navaho Medicine Man, Sandpaintings and Legends of Miguelito.* New York: J.J. Augustin.

1940 *Agentive and Causative Elements in Navaho.* New York: J.J. Augustin.

1943 Good Stories. *Journal of American Folklore* 56(219):69–71.

1944 *The Story of the Navaho Hail Chant.* New York: Barnard College.

1944 Prayer: The Compulsive Word. *American Ethnological Society Monograph* No. 7.

1948 Navaho Classification of Natural Objects. *Plateau* 21(1):7–12.

1949 "I, Personally." *The Atlantic,* July 13, 1949.

1950 *Navaho Religion, A Study of Symbolism.* New York: Pantheon.

1950 Another Look at the Navajo. Unpublished manuscript, Gladys Reichard Papers, Museum of Northern Arizona.

1951 Navaho Grammar. *American Ethnological Society Monograph* No. 21.

ROEDIGER, VIRGINIA M.

1941 *Ceremonial Costumes of the Pueblo Indians.* Berkeley, California: University of California Press.

SHEPARD, ANNA O.

n.d. Archaeological Ceramic Technology: Present Methods and Future Prospects. Anna Shepard Archives D9F7, University of Colorado Museum.

1936 Cell-Tempered Pottery. *American Antiquity* 2(2):137–139.

1936 Technology of Pecos Pottery. In The Pottery of Pecos. Vol. II. (with A.V. Kidder). *Papers of the Phillips Academy Southwestern Expedition* 7. Andover, Massachusetts, 389–587.

1938 Technical Notes on the Pottery of Unshagi. Appendix to *The Jemez Pueblo of Unshagi, New Mexico* Part 2:205–211. Albuquerque, New Mexico: University of New Mexico Press.

1939 Technology of La Plata Pottery. Appendix to Archaeological Studies in the La Plata District. *Carnegie Institution of Washington Publication* No. 519.

1942 Rio Grande Glaze Paint Ware. *Carnegie Institution of Washington Publication* No. 526, Contribution 39.

1948 The Symmetry of Abstract Design, with Specific Reference to Ceramic Decoration. *Carnegie Institution of Washington Publication* No. 574.

1950 Technological Notes on Mesa Verde Pottery. In Excavations in Mesa Verde National Park 1947–1948. *Medallion Papers* 39. Globe, Arizona, 89–91, 93–98.

1956 *Ceramics for the Archaeologist.* Carnegie Institution of Washington Publication No. 609.

1965 Rio Grande Glaze-Paint Pottery: A Test of Petrographic Analysis. In *Ceramics and Man,* ed. Frederick R. Matson. Viking Fund Publications in Anthropology No. 41.

SHEPARDSON, MARY T.

1963 Navajo Ways in Government: A Study in Political Process. *Memoirs of the American Anthropological Association* No. 96.

1964 Change and Persistence in an Isolated Navajo Community. (with Blodwen Hammond) *American Anthropologist* 66(5):1029–1050.

1965 Problems of the Navajo Tribal Courts in Transition. *Human Organization* 24(3):250–253.

1966 Navajo Inheritance Patterns: Random or Regular? (with Blodwen Hammond) *Ethnology* 5(1):87–96.

1970 *The Navajo Mountain Community: Social*

Organization and Kinship Terminology. (with Blodwen Hammond) Berkeley, California: University of California Press.

1971 Navajo Factionalism and the Outside World. In *Apachean Culture and Ethnology,* ed. Keith H. Basso and Morris E. Opler. *Anthropological Papers of the University of Arizona* No. 21:83–90.

1977 The Navajo Nonstate Nation. In *Nonstate Nations in International Politics: Comparative Systems Analyses*. ed. Judy S. Bertelsen. New York: Praegar.

1980 Foreword, *A Voice in Her Tribe: A Navajo Woman's Own Story,* by Irene Stewart. Socorro, New Mexico: Ballena Press.

1982 The Status of Navajo Women. *American Indian Quarterly* 6(1/2):149–169.

1982 Changing Attitudes toward Navajo Religion. In *Navajo Religion and Culture: Selected Views*. ed. David M. Brugge and Charlotte J. Frisbie. Santa Fe, New Mexico: Museum of New Mexico.

1986 *Fieldwork among the Navajo*. Palo Alto, California: BAS Press.

SPICER, ROSAMOND B.

1937 The Religious Participation of Yaqui Children. *Parent Teacher Journal of the New Church* 8(3):1–10.

1949 *The Desert People: A Study of the Papago Indians of Southern Arizona.* (with Alice Joseph and Jane Chesky) Chicago, Illinois: University of Chicago Press.

in press The Yaqui Easter Ceremony. In *A Yaqui Point of View: On Yaqui Ceremonies and Anthropologists*. ed. Richard Schechner. Cambridge and New York: Cambridge University Press.

Assistance on publications of Edward B. Spicer, including:

1947 Yaqui Villages Past and Present. *The Kiva* 13(1):1–12.

1954 Potam: A Yaqui Village in Sonora. *Memoirs of the American Anthropological Association* No. 77.

1962 *Cycles of Conquest: The Impact of Spain, Mexico, and the United States on the Indians of the Southwest, 1533–1960*. Tucson, Arizona: The University of Arizona Press.

1980 *The Yaquis: A Cultural History.* Tucson, Arizona: The University of Arizona Press.

STEVENSON, MATILDA COXE

1881 *Zuni and the Zunians*. Washington: privately printed.

1885 The Organization and Constitution of the Women's Anthropological Society. National Anthropological Archives, Smithsonian Institution.

1887 Religious Life of the Zuni Child. *5th Annual Report of the Bureau of Ethnology for 1883–1884:* 533–555.

1888 Zuni Religion. *Science* 11(268):136–137.

1894 The Sia. *11th Annual Report of the Bureau of Ethnology for 1889–1890:* 3–157.

1898 Zuni Ancestral Gods and Masks. *American Anthropologist* 11(1):33–40.

1904 The Zuni Indians: Their Mythology, Esoteric Fraternities, and Ceremonies. *23rd Annual Report of the Bureau of American Ethnology for 1901–1902:* 1–608.

1915 Ethnobotany of the Zuni Indians. *30th Annual Report of the Bureau of American Ethnology for 1908–1909:* 2–102.

1915 The Sun and Ice People among the Tewa Indians of New Mexico. *Smithsonian Miscellaneous Collections* 65(6):73–78.

TANNER, CLARA LEE

1935 They Live by Turquoise. *Arizona Highways* 11(3):3–5.

1935 Tanque Verde Ruins. *The Kiva* 1(4):1–4.

1943 Life Forms in Prehistoric Pottery of the Southwest. *The Kiva* 8(4):26–32.

1946 Apache Basketry. *Arizona Highways* 22(8):38–39.

1948 Ancient Pottery. *Arizona Highways* 24(2):36–39.

1950 Ventana Cave Textiles. In *The Stratigraphy of Archaeology of Ventana Cave, Arizona* by Emil W. Haury. Tucson, Arizona: The University of Arizona Press, 443–459.

1957 *Southwest Indian Painting*. Tucson, Arizona: The University of Arizona Press.

1960 The Influence of the White Man on Southwest Indian Art. *Ethnohistory* 7(2):137–150.

1968 *Southwest Indian Craft Arts*. Tucson, Arizona: The University of Arizona Press.

1976 Indians Arts and Crafts, special issue editor. *Arizona Highways*.

1976 *Prehistoric Southwestern Craft Arts*. Tucson, Arizona: The University of Arizona Press.

1978 The Squash Blossom. *American Indian Art Magazine* 3(3):36–43.

1982 *Apache Indian Baskets*. Tucson, Arizona: The University of Arizona Press.

1984 *Indian Baskets of the Southwest*. Tucson, Arizona: The University of Arizona Press.
1985 Southwest Indian Gold Jewelry. *The Kiva* 50(4):201–08.

TEIWES, HELGA
1967 *Excavations at Snaketown*. Documentary Film.
1969 *Mission San Xavier del Bac*. Documentary Film.
1973 *Mission San Xavier del Bac*. (text by Bernard L. Fontana). Tucson, Arizona: The University of Arizona Press.
1974 *Indians of Arizona*, ed. Thomas Weaver. Tucson, Arizona: The University of Arizona Press. (photographs)
1976 *The Hohokam: Desert Farmers and Craftsmen*. by Emil Haury. Tucson, Arizona: The University of Arizona Press. (photographs)
1976 *Prehistoric Southwestern Craft Arts*. by Clara Lee Tanner. Tucson, Arizona: The University of Arizona Press. (photographs)
1979 *The Material World of the Tarahumara*. (text by Bernard L. Fontana) Tucson, Arizona: The Arizona State Museum.
1979 *Handbook of North American Indians*. Vol. 9: Southwest, ed. Alfonso Ortiz. Washington, D.C.: Smithsonian Institution Press. (photographs)
1981 *Desert Plants: Papago Saguaro Fruit Harvest*. Tucson, Arizona: The University of Arizona Press.
1983 *Desert Plants: The Desert Tepary as a Food Source. Dry Farming*. (text by Frank Crosswhite) Tucson, Arizona: The University of Arizona Press.
1983 *Handbook of North American Indians*. Vol. 10, ed. Alfonso Ortiz. Washington, D.C.: Smithsonian Institution Press. (photographs)

THOMPSON, LAURA M.
1944 Some Perspectives in Applied Anthropology. *Applied Anthropology* 3(3):12–16.
1944 *The Hopi Way*. (with Alice Joseph) Chicago, Illinois: University of Chicago Press.
1945 Logico-Aesthetic Integration in Hopi Culture. *American Anthropologist* 47(4):540–553.
1947 White Pressures on Indian Personality and Culture. (with Alice Joseph) *American Journal of Sociology* 53:17–22.
1948 Attitudes and Acculturation. *American Anthropologist* 50(2):200–215.
1950 Action Research Among American Indians. *Scientific Monthly* 70(1):34–40.
1950 *Culture in Crisis: A Study of the Hopi Indians*. New York: Harper.
1951 *Toward a Science of Mankind*. New York: McGraw-Hill.
1951 Perception Patterns in Three Indian Tribes. *Psychiatry* 14:255–263.
1969 *The Secret of Culture: Nine Community Studies*. New York: Random House.
1970 Exploring American Indian Communities in Depth. In *Women in the Field: Anthropological Experiences*, ed. Peggy Golde:47–66. Chicago, Illinois: Aldine, 47–66.
1976 An Appropriate Role for Post Colonial Applied Anthropology. *Human Organization* 35(1):1–7.

UNDERHILL, RUTH M.
1935 The Ethnobiology of the Papago Indians. (with Edward Castetter) *University of New Mexico Bulletin* No. 275.
1936 Autobiography of a Papago Woman. *Memoir of the American Anthropological Association* No. 46.
1938 A Papago Calendar Record. *University of New Mexico Anthropology Series* Vol. 2, No.5.
1938 *First Penthouse Dwellers in America*. New York: J.J. Augustin.
1938 *Singing for Power*. Berkeley, California: University of California Press.
1939 Social Organization of the Papago Indians. *Columbia University Contributions to Anthropology* No. 30.
1944 *Pueblo Crafts*. Phoenix, Arizona: Education Division, BIA.
1946 Papago Indian Religion. *Columbia University Contributions to Anthropology* No. 33.
1948 Ceremonial Patterns in the Greater Southwest. *American Ethnological Society Monograph* No. 13.
1951 *People of the Crimson Evening*. Phoenix, Arizona: Education Division, BIA.
1953 *Red Man's America: A History of Indians in the United States*. Chicago, Illinois: University of Chicago Press.
1956 *The Navajos*. Norman, Oklahoma: University of Oklahoma Press.
1961 *Indians of the Southwest*. Garden City, New York: Doubleday.
1979 *Rainhouse and Ocean Speeches for the Papago Year*. (with D. Lopez, J. Pancho,

and D. Lopez) American Tribal Religion No. 4. Flagstaff, Arizona: Museum of Northern Arizona Press.

1979 *Papago Woman* (revised and expanded edition of *Autobiography of a Papago Woman,* 1936). New York: Holt, Rinehart and Winston.

VELARDE, PABLITA (TSE TSAN)

1960 *Old Father, the Story Teller.* Globe, Arizona: Dale Stuart King.

WHEELWRIGHT, MARY C.

1932 Some Embroideries from New Mexico. *Bulletin of the Needle and Bobbin Club* 16(2):19–27.

1938 Tleji or Yeibechai Myth by Hosteen Klah. *Bulletin of the House of Navajo Religion* No. 1.

1940 Myth of Sontso (Big Star). *Museum of Navajo Ceremonial Art Bulletin* No. 2.

1942 Navajo Creation Myth: The Story of the Emergence. (with Hosteen Klah) *Navajo Religion Series* No. 1. Santa Fe, New Mexico: Museum of Navajo Ceremonial Art.

1945 Atsah and Yohe. *Museum of Navajo Ceremonial Art Bulletin* No. 3.

1946 Hail Chant and Water Chant. *Navajo Religion Series* No. 2. Santa Fe, New Mexico: Museum of Navajo Ceremonial Art.

1946 *Coyote Chant.* Santa Fe, New Mexico: Museum of Navajo Ceremonial Art.

1949 Emergence Myth According to the Hanelth-Nayhe or Upward-Reaching Rite. *Navajo Religion Series* No 3. Santa Fe, New Mexico: Museum of Navajo Ceremonial Art.

1950 Notes on Some Navajo Coyote Myths. *New Mexico Folklore Record* 4:17–19.

1956 A Study of Navajo Symbolism. (with Franc Newcomb and Stanley Fishler) *Papers of the Peabody Museum* 32(3). Cambridge, Massachusetts: Harvard University Press.

1958 Male Shooting Chant. *Museum of Navajo Ceremonial Art Bulletin* No. 7.

1961 *Texts of the Navajo Creation Chants.* (with David McAllester) Cambridge, Massachusetts: Harvard University Press.

WOOD, NANCY

1966 *Little Wrangler.* New York: Doubleday.

1972 *Hollering Sun.* New York: Simon and Schuster.

1974 *In This Proud Land: America 1935–1943 as Seen in the FSA Photographs.* (with Roy Stryker) New York: New York Graphic.

1974 *Many Winters.* New York: Doubleday.

1976 *The King of Liberty Bend.* New York: Harper and Row.

1977 *The Man Who Gave Thunder to the Earth.* New York: Doubleday.

1978 *The Grass Roots People.* (photographs and text) New York: Harper and Row.

1979 *War Cry on a Prayer Feather.* New York: Doubleday.

1980 *When Buffalo Free the Mountains.* (photographs and text) New York: Doubleday.

WOODBURY, NATHALIE F. S.

1962 A Study of Land Use on the Papago Indian Reservation. (with Richard Woodbury) *Report to the Bureau of Ethnic Research,* University of Arizona.

1964 The Changing Patterns of Papago Land Use. (with Richard Woodbury) *Actas y Memorias* 35th International Congress of Americanists, Mexico, 1962.

1965 Zuni Prehistory and El Morro National Monument. (with Richard Woodbury) *Southwestern Lore* 21:56–60.

1966 The Excavation of Hawikuh by Frederick Webb Hodge: Report of the Hendricks-Hodge Expedition, 1917–1923. (with Watson Smith and Richard Woodbury) *Museum of the American Indian,* Contributions 20. New York: Heye Foundation.

WORMINGTON, H. MARIE

1939 *Ancient Man in North America.* Popular Series No. 4. Denver, Colorado: Colorado Museum of Natural History.

1947 *Prehistoric Indians of the Southwest.* Denver, Colorado: Denver Museum of Natural History.

1948 A Proposed Revision of Yuma Point Terminology. *Proceedings* 18(2):3–19. Denver Museum of Natural History.

1951 *The Story of Pueblo Pottery.* (with Arminta Neal) Denver Museum of Natural History, Pictorial No. 2.

1955 A Reappraisal of the Fremont Culture, with a Summary of the Archaeology of the Northern Periphery. *Proceedings,* n.s., No. 1. Denver Museum of Natural History.

1962 A Survey of Early American Prehistory. *American Scientist* 50(1):230–42.

1966 *Ancient Hunters of the Far West.* (with

Malcolm Rogers, Emma Lou Davis, and Clark W. Brott) San Diego, California: Union-Tribune Pub.

1969 *Prehistoric Indians of the Southwest.* Popular Series No.7. Denver Museum of Natural History.

1983 Early Man in the New World: 1970–1983. In *Early Man in the New World,* edited by Richard Shutler, Jr. Beverly Hills, California: Sage.